THE CHRISTIAN VISION
The Truth That Sets Us Free

John Powell, S.J.

ThomasMore
A DIVISION OF TABOR PUBLISHING

Allen, Texas

ACKNOWLEDGMENTS

Scripture quotations designated (GNB) are from the *Good News Bible,* the Bible in Today's English Version. Copyright © American Bible Society, 1976. Used by permission.

Excerpts from Juan Arias, *The God I Don't Believe In,* copyright © 1973 by St. Meinrad Archabbey, Inc., St. Meinrad, Indiana, with the permission of the publisher, Abbey Press.

Continued on page 155

PHOTO CREDITS

Otto Baitz/SHOSTAL ASSOCIATES   Cover
Jean-Claude LeJeune   All text photos

Copyright © 1984 by John Powell, S.J.

Send all inquiries to:
Thomas More Publishing
200 East Bethany Drive
Allen, Texas 75002–3804

Library of Congress Catalog Card Number 83–073231

Printed in the United States of America

ISBN 0–88347–329–1

9 10 11 12 13   99 98 97 96 95

Contents

Introduction

My dear Sisters and Brothers:

Some people have told me that as they read my books in the sequence in which they were written, they can trace my own personal development. I am always happy to hear this because I do try to live out my insights before I write about them. Like all ideas, insights have to be tested, and wherever necessary modified, in the laboratory of life.

This present book is in fact an outgrowth and extension of my last, *Fully Human, Fully Alive.* However, there has been in the intervening years another step in my own personal growth and development which was not recorded in a book. It was recorded rather in the form of a workshop intended for groups of four or more persons, called *The Fully Alive Experience.* This twenty-hour seminar was designed to investigate the force of attitudes in shaping our lives. After a preliminary consideration, the participants are invited to study the ways in which distorted and crippling attitudes can be discovered. Next there is some experimentation and exercise in the most effective methods for changing such attitudes. And finally, there is a review of five basic attitudes, with special emphasis on the Christian outlook, as found in the life and teachings of Jesus.

The Fully Alive Experience was prepared and presented to more than ten thousand people by myself and Loretta Brady, who is a Couple and Family Christian Therapist. After offering our seminar in fifty cities of the United States, as well as in Europe, Australia, and New Zealand, Loretta and I decided that it was simply too effective and helpful to be shelved.

So we recorded the talks on eleven audiocassettes, and we published the Personal Notebook in which each participant processes the ideas presented. We also composed and published a Guidebook so groups could make *The Fully Alive Experience* on their own, with or without previous experience. Our hopes for the "packaged" version of *The Fully Alive Experience* have been realized even beyond our most optimistic expectations. We have received many notes of gratitude from groups of all kinds, attesting to the life-changing effectiveness of these twenty hours spent in attitudinal investigation and revision. For those who belong either to a growth or to a prayer group, and who might be interested, *The Fully Alive Experience* basic kit is available from Argus Communications, One DLM Park, Allen, Texas 75002. This basic kit of the eleven audiocassettes, a Personal Notebook, and the Guidebook can be ordered from Argus Communications either by mail or by telephone (call toll free 800-527-4747 or, in Texas, 800-442-4711).

This present book, *The Christian Vision,* is in its turn an outgrowth of *The Fully Alive Experience.* My input talks, as recorded in the packaged version of *The Fully Alive Experience,* are expanded here. In addition, other attitudes are investigated and presented from the Christian perspective. In this book I do not go into the detection of and methods for revising crippling attitudes. That was done more than adequately in *The Fully Alive Experience.*

It is a source of profound gratification to be able to share these insights, attitudes, and milestones of my own development with you. I am told that my eight books published by Argus Communications now have a circulation of more than eleven million copies. Even in my most technicolor, adolescent dreams I never anticipated anything like this. All I can say is that God has been very good to me and very gracious in using whatever I have to offer. I am likewise overwhelmed by the graciousness of my Christian sisters and brothers who have welcomed my words and wanted to share my thoughts. It has been a very consoling faith experience.

Recently I heard an appealing analogy for the faith experience. It seems that a small boy was flying a kite high up in the sky. Soon a low-drifting cloud encircled the kite and hid it from view. A man passing by asked the little boy what he was doing with that string in his hand. "Flying my kite," the child responded. The man looked up at the sky and saw only the cloud in an otherwise clear sky. "I don't see a kite up there. How can you be sure that there is a kite up there?" The child replied, "I don't see it either, but I know my kite is up there because every once in a while there is a little tug on the string."

In the same sense I know that there is a guiding hand in mine as I proceed along the path of my life. I know that there is a light, not mine, that shows me the way I am to go, one step at a time. I know that the Lord walks with me. And there is a deep and warm sense of gratitude in my heart to walk this way with you as my companion. With the Lord's guidance and your company, "every once in a while there is a little tug on the string." Thanks for letting me tell you about it.

Please remember me as loving you.

John Powell, S.J.

CHAPTER 1

The Vision:
What You See Is What You Get

"No one lights a lamp and then hides it or puts it under a bowl; instead, he puts it on the lampstand, so that people may see the light as they come in. Your eyes are like a lamp for the body. When your eyes are sound, your whole body is full of light; but when your eyes are no good, your whole body will be in darkness. Make certain, then, that the light in you is not darkness. If your whole body is full of light, with no part of it in darkness, it will be bright all over, as when a lamp shines on you with its brightness." Luke 11:33-36 (GNB)

A Snake on Your Lawn

May I ask you to run a short homemade movie on the screen of your imagination? Imagine that you come home some dark night and, to your horror, you see a thirty-five foot snake on your front lawn. Your heart begins to pound wildly and adrenalin starts pumping into your blood-stream. You quickly grab a garden hoe and in your frenzy you hack the writhing snake into small pieces. Satisfied that it is dead, you go inside and try to settle your nerves with a warm drink. Later, lying in bed, even with your eyes closed, you can still see the wriggling form on the front lawn.

The next morning you return to the scene of the snake slaying and find, again to your horror, that there had never been a snake on your front lawn. That which lies in pieces before your eyes was simply the garden hose which had been left out on the lawn. It was always a hose, of course; but last night for you it was a snake. What you saw last night was a snake, and all your actions and reactions followed from what you saw. The fear, the hoe, the struggle, the effort to calm down—all followed from the vision of a thirty-five foot snake. (The end of our homemade movie. Please turn on the house lights.)

What this exercise of imagination was meant to illustrate is that all our emotional and behavioral actions and reactions follow from our percep-tions. In the snake drama, we were talking about the perceptions of an ocular vision, about a vision seen with the eyes of the body. But we also have an inner vision of reality, a highly personal and unique way that each one of us perceives reality—a vision seen with the eyes of the mind. We look at the various parts of reality through the eyes of our minds, and no two people ever see those parts of reality in exactly the same way. You have your vision. I have mine.

The important fact is this: We always act and react according to what we see. If I see a thirty-five foot snake—even though it is really a garden hose—my glands and my emotions, my hands and feet and palpitating heart all react to the "snake" I see.

And so, the way we see things shapes the kinds of experiences we have. For example, if I see you coming toward me and I perceive you in my mind's eye as a dear friend, a warm feeling will come over me, a smile will light up my face. I will reach out to shake your hand or to embrace you. However, if I see you approaching me and I perceive you as hostile, intent on hurting or robbing me, my physical, emotional, and behavioral reactions will be just the opposite. It all depends on how I see or perceive you.

There was an old Roman philosopher, Epictetus, who lived shortly after our Lord. I don't suppose the man or his message was too popular, but he kept saying to the people, "It isn't your problems that are bothering you. It is the way you are looking at them. It's all in the way you look at things!" Epictetus may not have been revered for repeating this refrain, but, you know, I think he was right. It is all in the way we see or look at things. One thirsty person can look at a half-filled glass of water and gleefully observe, "Oh, good! It's half full." Another thirsty person might well look at the same glass and dejectedly moan, "Oh, nuts! It's half empty." We all remember the rhyming couplet: "Two men looked out from prison bars. One saw mud, the other stars." It's all in the way we look at it. Ultimately, all of our lives are shaped by our perceptions, by the way we look at things.

Perceptions and Attitudes

There are many things that we perceive again and again in very much the same way. Pretty soon such repeated perceptions get to be a habit. For example, it may be that a certain man has always perceived money as very important. He can never forget the day he lost a dime in first grade, or the day he collected his first paycheck. Whenever this man made money, won money, found money, he was greatly elated and congratulated himself. But whenever he spent money or lost money, he felt very dejected. This way of looking at money, after it has been repeated many times, becomes a habit. The man in question has an habitual way of perceiving the reality of money: It is very important and looms very large in his vision. And this is what I call an attitude. Our lives are shaped and governed by our attitudes.

Up in your head and mine are thousands of these attitudes. Sometimes I think of them as the lenses of the mind through which each of us sees reality in his or her own way. These lenses can shrink or magnify, color, clarify or obscure the reality seen through them. And there is a different lens for every different part of reality. Some of us magnify certain things and diminish others, but no two of us ever see anything in exactly the same way. What is most important, I think, is that our actions and reactions are determined by something inside us, by the way we see reality, by our attitudes.

Our attitudes are truly the lenses of the mind through which we perceive reality. However, there is another comparison which helps me more fully understand the force of attitudes. I imagine our attitudes as jurors sitting in the jury box of the mind, poised and ready to interpret all the evidence that is brought before them. These juror-attitudes are ready to pronounce verdicts and to suggest appropriate actions and reactions. For example, I look into the mirror and I see new wrinkles or gray hairs: unmistakable evidence that I am growing old. This evidence, coming through my senses, reaches my mind. There the proper and duly appointed juror—my attitude toward aging—rises, evaluates the evidence, makes a pronouncement, and suggests an appropriate reaction.

Perhaps the juror-attitude quotes Robert Browning: "Grow old along with me! / The best is yet to be, / The last of life for which the first was made. / Our times are in his hand." ("Rabbi Ben Ezra") Browning's own attitude suggests that the most appropriate reaction would be a sense of satisfaction, and would perhaps result in a serene smile which results from the reflection that "these are the best of times . . ."

Or the juror-attitude could be very different. It could quote Dylan Thomas: "Do not go gentle into that good night, / Old age should burn and rave at close of day; / Rage, rage against the dying of the light." ("Do Not Go Gentle into That Good Night") Such an attitude seems to interpret the evidence harshly and angrily, even to the point of suggesting that the appropriate response would be a disappointed frustration and rebellion. "Just when I get over the hump, I'm also over the hill! And it had to happen during the Pepsi generation when you're supposed to 'think young!'" If this is my attitude, I might well walk away from the mirror, dejectedly thinking about a facelift or a hair rinse.

It all depends on the way I look at the process of aging. It all depends on the lens through which I look at aging. It all depends on the juror-attitude toward aging in my mind. The important thing that we must observe and absorb until it really sinks in is that our attitudes shape our reactions, emotional as well as behavioral. Our attitudes are capable of making the same given experience either pleasant or painful. They can make of the same experience either a constructive challenge to grow or a destructive catastrophe.

Sometimes in my university classroom, I try this experiment to illustrate the same point. I ask my students, "If one of you suddenly stood up and stamped angrily out of this classroom, reading me out and writing me off, how would I react? How would I feel? What would I say or do?"

My classes have always been eager to respond. Usually one student says, "You would be very *angry*. You would say, 'Get that person's name and number. He's not going to get away with this!'" Another student suggests, "No, you would probably feel *hurt*. You'd wonder, 'How could you do this to me? I was doing the best I could.'" Still another member of the class usually proposes, "You would probably feel *guilty,* and would accuse yourself of failing. You would want to apologize, and would wonder what you had done wrong. 'What did I do? I must have said something that infuriated that person. Hey, come back; I'm really sorry!'" I usually find one of my students who suggests, "You'd feel *compassionate,* sorry for the angry, departing person. You'd say something like 'Poor fella! He just isn't ready for this yet.'"

I am always pleased to have these various and different reactions. Actually, I think that each suggestion is a projection of the attitude (and consequent reactions) of the suggester. We tend to think that everybody would react to given situations just as we do, but this just isn't true. Our attitudes are always unique. By the way, if you are wondering, I'm not sure how I would react. Whenever someone walks out on me, I always presume that he or she is going to use the washroom. The fact is that I might well react in any of the suggested ways. However, this I know: My reactions would reflect my attitudes—my attitude toward myself and my presentation, my attitude toward rejection by others, and perhaps my attitude about the necessity of pleasing others. These would be the jurors that would pass a verdict on the situation and dictate to me an appropriate response.

The central and critical realization is that my reaction, whatever it might be, is not determined by the person walking out on me, but by something inside me. My reaction is determined by my own inner attitudes. *A* reaction can be *stimulated* by thousands of things, but *my specific* reaction is *determined* by the way I perceive the person or thing or situation which is stimulating a reaction in me. It all depends on the jurors in the court of my mind, on the lenses over my mind. The juror-attitude in the court of my mind will inevitably interpret, judge, and suggest an appropriate reaction.

So when I wonder about my emotional and behavioral reactions to life and its events, I have to investigate my own inner attitudes. It is completely counterproductive to take inventory of someone else's attitudes rather than my own. If I resort to blaming others, I will never learn much about myself. It is futile to ask, What got into him? Instead, if I wish to grow, I have to confront the question, How am I looking at this? I have to realize that something in me passes judgment, dictates my reactions, and makes the experience growthful or embittering.

From where I now stand I would say that this is the essential difference between a growing and a nongrowing person. If I am willing to see my reactions as a reflection of my own inner attitudes, I am definitely moving toward self-knowledge and human maturity. Of course, I would rather blame my negative reactions on someone else or on something else. I might even resort to blaming the position of the stars: "My moon just wasn't in the right house!" However, if I give in to this temptation, I will be stunting my own growth as a person. "The fault, dear Brutus, is not with our stars, but with ourselves . . ." (Shakespeare, *Julius Caesar*) The initial and essential step toward full human maturity is the honest and gutsy admission that I am acting and reacting because of something in myself: my own habitual way of perceiving persons, things, situations. All my reactions are the result of my inner attitudes.

Attitudes in Action

In my book *Fully Human, Fully Alive,* I told the story of the sudden death of a car which I was driving on a busy Chicago expressway. Standing on the shoulder of the expressway, alongside the unresponsive automobile, I glanced down into the ravine on one side of the expressway, noting the high fence and dense foliage at the bottom. Looking out across the expressway, I was faced in that direction with six lanes of whizzing traffic. The result in me was instant panic. I did not know what to do. What I did not reveal about this episode in that other book was that several months later a woman who works with me (Loretta Brady) came late for a meeting. "Sorry," she said, "my car broke down." I made sympathetic enquiries only to find out that her car broke down at the very same place where my own tragedy occurred. (Shades of the "Bermuda Triangle!") I know it sounds a bit contrived, but it is actually true.

"What did you do?"

"I climbed down the hill on the west side of the expressway!" she chirped with a slightly triumphal smile.

"Isn't there a big fence at the bottom of that hill?"

"Yes, I climbed over it!" (The triumphal smile widening)

"You did! Then what?"

"I went under the overpass, found a phone, and called for help."

(Long, painful pause)

"Could I ask you a personal question: How did you feel when you were doing all this?"

(So help me God) "Exhilarated!"

(So help me God) "Oh, I hate you!"

As you can tell, I like to repeat this story, mostly for my own benefit. What the incident drives home for me is that my inner attitudes—the lenses, the jurors—determine the nature of my experiences and ultimately make my life happy or unhappy, pleasurable or painful, exhilarating or panic-filled. I really need to absorb and remember this. In order to remind myself of this crucial realization, I have a sign in my mirror (the first thing I see every morning) which reads: "You are looking at the face of the person who is responsible for your happiness today!" It's all in the way we look at it, Epictetus! I presume that this truth is what Abraham Lincoln had in mind when he said in one of his most quoted statements: "People are about as happy as they decide they are going to be." It also seems to be what William Cowper, the poet, had in mind when he wrote: "Happiness depends, as Nature shows, / Less on exterior things than most suppose." ("Table Talk")

You must have heard the story—and it is just a story—of the identical twin boys. One was a hopeless optimist: "Everything is coming up roses!" The other boy was a sad and hopeless pessimist. He was sure that Murphy, as in "Murphy's Law," was an optimist. The worried parents of the boys brought them to the local psychologist. He suggested to the parents of the boys a plan to level the boys off. "On their next birthday, put them in separate rooms to open their birthday gifts. Give the pessimist the best toys you can afford, and give the optimist a box of manure." The parents followed these instructions (remember, this is only a fable) and carefully observed the results. When they peeked in on the pessimist, they heard him audibly complaining:

"I don't like the color of this computer . . . I'll bet this calculator will break . . . I don't like this game . . . I know someone who's got a bigger toy car than this . . ."

Tiptoeing across the corridor, the parents peeked in and saw their little optimist gleefully throwing the manure up in the air. He was giggling:

"You can't fool me! Where there's this much manure, there's gotta be a pony!"

The story is meant to illustrate that it's all in the way we look at things. And it all depends on what we are looking for, because we inevitably find that which we are looking for. The optimist looks for and expects to find the brighter side, the silver lining, the hopeful, the good things that are so often buried in the brambles of life. Very often the most magnificent opportunities come into our lives disguised as problems. Only the eyes that search for such opportunities can find them. The pessimist is deprived of all these advantages because he looks for and usually finds the things that can go wrong.

The Good News: We Can Change Attitudes

The good news is, of course, that we are free to change our attitudes and consequently our lives. Attitudes are no more than practiced or habitual ways of perceiving some part of reality. We can break old habits and make new ones. We can drop in, over the eyes of our minds, a different set of lenses. We can retrain our mental jurors. We can look for and find a new and brighter outlook, and consequently enjoy a fuller and happier life.

The great William James was a Harvard-trained physician and professor. He soon discovered in his medical investigations that a person's outlook or way of seeing things has a profound influence on physical health. He realized that most of the patients who consulted him with a physical complaint really needed a revision of outlook. So James took up the study of psychology and eventually wrote a minor masterpiece called *The Principles of Psychology*. In this book Dr. James wrote: "The greatest discovery in our generation is that human beings, by changing the inner attitudes of their minds, can change all the outer aspects of their lives."

As you know, this same William James has written many books on religion and the advancement of human spiritual frontiers. In these books James repeatedly insists that our happiness depends not so much on what happens *to* us as on what happens *in* us. When we meet life and its circumstances positively and triumphantly, then no matter what comes we will have learned the master secret of living. The way we see, interpret, and react to whatever happens to us is the important thing. Sometimes the very worst thing that may happen *to* us can bring about the best thing that could ever happen *in* us. And we must assume this responsibility for what happens in us. We must assume responsibility for our attitudes. Only if we accept this responsibility can we grow through the various circumstances of life. This was the message of William James.

Psychiatric Testimony

More recently a psychiatrist at the University of Pennsylvania, Dr. David D. Burns, has written a testimony to the same truth. In his excellent book *Feeling Good: The New Mood Therapy*, psychiatrist Burns reminds us that everything depends on our perceptions, the way we see things. He insists that we always feel and act the way we think; our attitudes shape all that follows from them. If our attitudes are distorted and crippling, our thinking is illogical and dysfunctional. In this condition we soon begin to experience a whole range of burdensome, oppressive emotions, and these are reflected in our behavior. The monkeys on our backs are really born in our minds. Our distorted perceptions become our merciless tyrants. We become the tortured prisoners of these crippling attitudes, which will torment us as long as we tolerate them.

Another psychiatrist, the well-known Viktor Frankl, is basically teaching the same thing in his system of "Logotherapy." A former student of Frankl's, Dr. Robert C. Leslie, author of *Jesus and Logotherapy*, recalls these words from a conversation with Dr. Frankl: "Everybody can be helped, if not directly by psychoanalytic approaches, then indirectly by helping the patient to change his attitude." Leslie then adds by way of explanation:

> The tendency in medical circles is so to focus attention on the symptom that the underlying attitude is lost sight of. It is the assumption

of Logotherapy, however, that many symptoms (although, obviously not all) are the direct result of unhealthy attitudes, and that often relief can be accomplished by changing the attitude rather than by treating the symptom. . . .

It is to be noted that in so focusing the attention on the attitude and away from the symptom, attention is directed to the future rather than to the past. The implication is that whatever the conditions have been in the past that caused the symptoms, the important factor is not so much the uncovering of an underlying conflict responsible for the symptom as it is the adoption of an attitude which makes possible a handling of the symptom.[1]

In his own, best-known book, *Man's Search for Meaning,* Dr. Frankl writes:

Logotherapy is neither teaching nor preaching. It is as far removed from logical reasoning as it is from moral exhortation. To put it figuratively, the role played by the Logotherapist is rather that of an eye-specialist than that of a painter. A painter tries to convey to us a picture of the world as he sees it; an ophthalmologist tries to enable us to see the world as it really is. The Logotherapist's role consists in widening and broadening the visual fields of the patient so that the whole spectrum of meaning and values becomes conscious and visible to him.[2]

Still another of the great psychiatrists, Dr. Carl G. Jung, writes in his book *The Practice of Psychotherapy,* "The task of psychotherapy is to correct the conscious attitudes and not to chase after infantile memories."

What Drs. Burns, Frankl, Leslie, and Jung are saying is that we are fully free only when the lenses of our attitudes allow us to see reality clearly, only when we can find meaning and value in ourselves, in our fellow human beings, in life and in death. Very often we encounter people who sound as though they have swallowed a *mechanistic* view of humans. We hear people say resignedly, "This is the way I am. It was this way in the beginning, is now and ever shall be." They seem to be saying that when human beings are stimulated in a given way, the response is automatic and mechanical, and in no way free. Such people do not seem to be aware of the possibility of seeing things differently, of cultivating new attitudes. They do not seem to acknowledge the hope-filled truth that we can break old and crippling habits of perception and cultivate new, life-giving habits.

---

[1] Robert C. Leslie, *Jesus and Logotherapy* (Nashville: Abingdon Press, 1965), p. 94.
[2] Viktor Frankl, *Man's Search for Meaning* (New York: Washington Square Press, 1969), p. 174.

A (Saintly) Example of the Above

When I am thinking about the force and effects of our attitudes, I often think of the life and especially of the death of one of my favorite role models, Sir Thomas More, lawyer and saint. For me, this man is a living refutation of the mechanistic, the-way-it-is thesis. His living and especially his dying are a testimony to the effect of our attitudes on our reactions. Coming face to face with death usually strips us of our pretenses. Death is the ultimate test of attitudes, I would think. The humor of Thomas More going to his death by decapitation has always impressed me very deeply. It is reported that his last words to his doleful executioner were a request for a little help up the stairs of the execution platform. Sir Thomas More assured the poor man that he could take care of himself coming down. "See me safe up. For my coming down I can shift for myself." And he is said to have added, "And let us pray for each other so that we will all meet merrily in heaven."

To me this man's dying is more than a triumph of virtue, which it certainly was. It is also a marvelous illustration of a Christian attitude toward death and honor. As you remember, More was dying as a matter of principle and conscience. He once compared personal honor to water cupped in one's hands. "Once you spread your fingers even slightly, it is difficult to recapture your honor." When I grow up (attitudinally), I want to turn out like Thomas More.

All that we have been saying about the radical role of attitudes in shaping our lives is generally known and accepted by psychology. The way we perceive reality through the lenses of our attitudes has a profound influence on our emotional, physical, and relational health. Our attitudes release or constrict the use of our abilities, and they color our personalities. Great minds from Epictetus to Viktor Frankl seem to insist on this. However, what our philosophers, psychologists, and psychiatrists do not have within their scientific resources is a master vision, a vision to which we can compare our own in an effort to locate our distortions and to acquire the healthy attitudes that will help us to live and to die as fully alive people like Thomas More. This is the precise significance of the Word of God, as it comes to us in the person and vision of Jesus. Jesus offers us just such a master vision.

However, before we consider this master vision of Jesus, we must first ask ourselves a question.

CHAPTER 2

What's in Me?

Jesus took the blind man by the hand and led him out of the village. . . . Jesus placed his hands on him and asked him, "Can you see anything?" The man looked up and said, "Yes, I can see people, but they look like trees walking around." Jesus again placed his hands on the man's eyes. This time the man looked intently, his eyesight returned, and he saw everything clearly.   Mark 8:23-25 (GNB)

Asking the Right Question

The crucial insight and realization, which opens up a whole new dimension of personal growth, is this: Something in me—my attitudes, my vision of reality—determines all my actions and reactions, both emotional and behavioral. Something in me is writing the story of my life, making it sad and sorrowful or glad and peaceful. Something in me will ultimately make the venture of my life a success or a failure. The sooner I acknowledge this, taking responsibility for my actions and reactions, the faster I will move toward my destiny: the fullness of life and peace. This fullness of life and peace is our legacy from the Lord.

I must not let this remain a matter of words, a lip-service admission. I must ask myself if in fact I really believe this. Am I really convinced that my inner attitudes evaluate the persons, events, and situations of my life and regulate all my reactions? If so, I must press on and ask, Do I truly believe that it is within my power to change these attitudes, wherever necessary, in order to have a full and meaningful life? If I find that I am convinced on both scores, then I must close all the escape-from-reality doors and walk bravely down the corridor of personal responsibility. I must resist the ever-present temptation to blame other people, to complain about the past and present circumstances of my life, including the weather and the position of the stars. In a true sense, I must become "the master of my fate," and under God take the responsibility for my own happiness.

Consequently, the key and profitable question is not: Will this day bring me my desires? It is not: Will I get the breaks? Nor is it: How can I change all these people who surround me and shackle me and carry me along in the stream of their movement? The only key and profitable question is this: What is in me? It is not, as we heard William James insist, what happens *to* me but rather what happens *in* me that will shape, color, and write the story of my life.

15

Now I don't think that you and I should think that we have to begin tearing down all the bricks of our existing mental structures. I rather suppose, in fact, that most of our attitudes are reasonable and healthy. We probably suffer from only several distorted attitudes. Also, we should recognize that the few which do pinch and prove painful have somewhere along the course of our lives been learned from others. Even though we were not always correctly understanding what they were saying, we did learn our first, inherited attitudes from our parents. Of course, there is no question of blame here, only of understanding.

Discomfort and the Need for Change

When these supposedly few neurotic attitudes actively distort our vision and cripple our responses, the result is always some form of DISCOMFORT! This discomfort can be (1) *physical:* We get tense and develop a headache or a skin rash, or we experience a knot or nausea in the stomach. We might come down with frequent head colds and find ourselves susceptible to various viruses. The discomfort can also be (2) *emotional:* We might frequently feel ill at ease, intimidated, anxious, inferior, guilty, depressed, angry and upset, afraid, frustrated, and so forth. Finally, the discomfort can be (3) *behavioral:* In this case we feel uncomfortable in the recognition of our own undesirable behavior. Examples: For a long time I have refused to talk to someone, or I don't tell others how I really feel. I pout and punish others by my silence. I pretend to be happy, but inside I know that it is just an act; actually I am hurting badly. I am immobilized; I haven't been able to do anything for several days now. Or I can't seem to make and keep friends. I am not able to tell others that I love them, even when I really do care very much for them. All of these, I would think, are behavioral symptoms of crippling and distorted attitudes.

The symptomatic discomfort, then, is reflected either physically, emotionally, or behaviorally, or perhaps in all three ways at the same time. Most of the time the discomfort is in fact experienced in all three ways. However, some of us are more aware of what our bodies are telling us. Others among us are better at listening to feelings or emotions. And finally, there are many of us who are not very good at physical or emotional awareness, but we do know that things are just not right with the way we are acting, reacting, and relating to others.

It is extremely important that we do not run away from our discomfort, but rather enter into and examine it. The discomfort is a signal, a teacher offering us a valuable lesson. The way we enter into our discomfort profitably and find the source of our difficulty is usually by asking, What is in me? I must ask myself, How am I looking at myself, at this other person, at this situation? My physical, emotional, and behavioral reactions are ultimately a result of my outlook. They are an outgrowth of my attitudes. In most moments of discomfort, I am feeling the effect of my attitudes in my body, in my feelings, in my actions and reactions. It is very important that I trace this discomfort to its cause:

16

What is in me? How am I perceiving myself, another, this circumstance? The honest answering of these questions will explain my bodily, emotional, and behavioral reactions.

After I have located the attitude in question, then I must ask another question: Is there a different way to see myself, to see this other person or this situation? Can I think of a way that would be more realistic, healthier, more Christian? I must reflect that there are other people who would somehow remain peaceful, optimistic, gentle, and unruffled if they were in my shoes at this time. How would they perceive this moment and circumstance in my life if they were me? How would Jesus suggest that I look at myself, at this other person, at this situation?

The Process of Change: Case Examples

Examples of this process, like life situations, are innumerable. But let's examine a few cases here, and then perhaps we can outline others from our own life situations.

CASE #1 (awareness of a distorted attitude through physical discomfort): I am tense and nervous. The back of my head and neck ache. I know that these physical reactions almost always occur when I am in a classroom. Sometimes I react this way just before an examination, or when I am in some other way being tested and evaluated. I don't test very well because I always "choke" during examinations. Basically, I suppose that the emotion which stimulates these physical reactions is fear. I am really afraid that I will be called on or tested and I will reveal my ignorance in some stupid statement. I dread the very thought of such failure and embarrassment. Failing at anything is always very torturous for me. It is like being hit again in a place that is already bruised. I am always tense and nervous at the thought that I will be found wanting and inadequate.

Diagnosis of distortion: In the last analysis, each of us must become aware of his or her own individual discomfort and come to his or her own conclusions. Only Cinderella can tell if the shoe really fits or where it hurts. However, we can speculate that the attitude underlying the physical discomfort described here has to do with the way this person sees himself or herself. This person seems to perceive his or her personal worth as measured by ready knowledge and intelligence and by the judgment of public opinion. People who measure themselves in this way see themselves as slaves standing on the auction block, hearing their worth estimated by the public bidders. They are indeed slaves, enslaved by the fear that others will test and reject them. They are slaves of the attitude that a person's intrinsic worth is measured by achievement and by the recognition of others.

In search of an alternative attitude: Having located the source of the physical tension in this attitude, the uncomfortable person should reflect that there are others who do not seem to be affected in this way.

The reflection might sound something like this: "There are others who aren't even as smart as I am who actually seem to enjoy class and who seem to be able to take examinations in stride. There are those who don't go into a tailspin, as I do, when they make a public mistake. There are even some who can laugh at their own blunders. I wonder what these people are thinking. Apparently they look at these situations in which I experience so much physical discomfort very differently than I do."

Healthy attitude: It is always crippling to play the comparison game, comparing my looks, my brains, or my accomplishments with those of others. The comparison game is the sure way to a poor self-image. The truth is that I am the one and only me! Furthermore, all people are mistake-makers. We humans learn by trial and error. We learn by making mistakes and learning from them. Besides, the only real mistake is the one from which we learn nothing. Thomas Edison tried two thousand different materials in search of a filament for the light bulb. When none worked satisfactorily, his assistant complained, "All our work is in vain. We have learned nothing." Edison replied very confidently, "Oh, we have come a long way and we have learned a lot. We now know that there are two thousand elements which we cannot use to make a good light bulb."

Comment: I know that I have correctly uncovered my sick and crippling attitude and that I have replaced it with a healthy vision if and when the physical discomfort of tension greatly subsides or disappears. The same thing is true with emotional or behavioral discomfort.

CASE #2 (awareness of a distorted attitude through emotional discomfort): I feel alone and lonely most of the time. It is like the whole human race is holding a picnic and I wasn't invited. It seems that the only way I can get any attention is by being needy, by bleeding all over the place. It is really very depressing. I guess I just haven't got it.

Diagnosis of distortion: A person who feels this way probably perceives himself or herself as unattractive and unlovable. Imprisoned by this perception of personal ugliness, such a person can pine away a lifetime, wishing to be better looking, more intelligent, wittier, and so forth. Many people see lovability in these terms. Actually, what makes a person attractive and lovable is being loving, truly caring about other people, going out to read and respond to the needs of others. The perpetually lonely person usually does not realize this.

In search of an alternative attitude: There are other people who don't feel as isolated and lonely as I do. Many of them do not seem to have a better natural endowment of gifts than I do. So what do they have that I don't? What do they do that I don't? How do they think of and approach social relationships? I really should ask them.

Healthy attitude: It is truly caring for others that makes a person lovable. And I have at least some capacity for this: to get out of myself, to go out in personal caring to try to meet the needs of others. A loving person is a lovable person. What I am is really what I do with what I've got. My isolation and estrangement are really self-imposed. I have been sitting in this dark room, waiting for someone to come in and light up my life. I have to get out, to read and respond to the needs of others around me. Only then will I present to others the lovable person that I truly am. If I go out to others in a sincere and consistent way, I will certainly be loved and appreciated. The bread of love always comes back on the waters of life.

CASE #3 (awareness of a distorted attitude through behavioral discomfort): It really bothers me that you can't trust anyone anymore, not even your own family. Sooner or later people let you down. They'll do it every time. I have given up on having heroes or models. Everybody I've ever looked up to turns out to have clay feet. Even the religious people who go to church all the time are in fact hypocrites. They don't practice what they preach. I'm so disgusted with people. I just try to avoid them as far as possible. I have become a loner. I say as little as I can to other people. There is no one I really trust. I feel safer this way.

Diagnosis of distortion: It would seem that this person gives strong indications that he or she is a demanding perfectionist, at least with regard to others but most probably also with regard to self. In the thinking of such a person, the norm by which all people must be judged is absolute perfection. However, as has been noted, people are mistake-makers. That is why we put erasers on pencils. Even Saint Paul complained, "I see the right thing, I approve it, and then I do just the opposite. There is another law warring in my members." (See Romans 7:14-25.) It is also true that we become angry at and disgusted with others only when our expectations have somehow been disappointed. If we entertain the expectation that everyone should be perfect, our lives will probably be very painful. The fact is that no one is perfect. So rather than try to pull the whole world up to our unrealistic expectations, it would be a much wiser course of action to lower our expectations and to realize that the human condition is one of weakness. And, with Saint Paul, all of us can truly say, "This is my condition, too."

Finally, the process of human maturity is a gradual process. None of us is ever really and fully "grown up." It would be an unrealistic expectation to demand this in ourselves or in others. We are pilgrims, always on the way, but never really there. "So please be patient," the sign reads, "God is not finished with me yet."

In search of an alternative attitude: There are others who live in the same world as I do. They cannot be blind to all the human frailties and imperfections that surround us and are a part of life on planet Earth. I wonder what they think when people disappoint them. They somehow seem to accept it and to go on. Their expectation of others is apparently not the same as mine. I will have to ask some of these people what they are thinking, how they cope, and how they manage to keep up real relationships of love. Above all, I want to know how they manage to forgive and to go right on, almost as though nothing had ever happened.

Healthy attitude: It is true that the human condition is one of weakness. Every human being experiences weakness, fragility, and brokenness. Every one of us has to live with personal regrets. The only pertinent and real questions are these: Can I accept myself and others in this human condition of weakness? Can I ever learn to take myself and other people where we are? If I lower my unrealistic expectations to meet the reality of the human condition, I will consequently be more pleased by the goodness that I find in people and less disappointed with the weakness that is in all of us.

Also, each of us finds what he or she is looking for. The person who looks for weakness will certainly find it, in the self and in others. However, there is a lot more to each of us than our weakness. Deep down, most of us are basically well-intentioned. But this isn't always obvious. Our intentions don't always come through in our actions. Still we usually mean well even if we can't always do well. In order to love, one need not be blind but rather supersighted. The loving person must look past the surface weaknesses and find the essential goodness in self and in others. However, this finding can come only to those who are looking, looking more for goodness than for weakness.

*   *   *

As mentioned, examples could go on endlessly. But it might be more helpful at this point for you to put the book down and work through some personal discomfort (physical, emotional, or behavioral) and see if you can uncover its attitudinal roots. Then see if you can articulate a healthy attitude to replace the unhealthy one.

The main points to be realized are these: Discomfort may often be a sign of a crippling or distorted attitude. Our way of looking at something shapes our reactions to that reality. If the reaction results in discomfort, this may be an indication that the reality is not being seen in its proper, Christian perspective. The discomfort may be physical, emotional, or behavioral; but whatever it is, the discomfort could be saying something to us that we really need to hear if we are to grow and to be happy, if we are to live the full and peaceful life for which we have been created.

I think it is important to realize that sometimes the experience of discomfort is *not* the result of a distorted attitude. There are very real human aches and pains that are a part of living and loving which do not imply or result from distorted attitudes. Allowing for this, I still think that ninety percent of our human discomfort is neurotic, that is, it results from a distorted and unrealistic way of seeing things. I think that ninety percent of our suffering is done on the way to the dentist and not in his chair. At any rate, when we are uncomfortable, we should always try to trace that discomfort to its attitudinal roots, to the way we are seeing things. After the attitude has been clearly recognized, we can then ask ourselves if this is a healthy and Christian way to see the reality in question. Is the discovered attitude one that I would want to recommend to another? Do I want to keep it for myself?

Among My Own Attitudes of Affliction

It has been said, and I truly believe it, that each of us harbors a core of several disjointed and crippling attitudes that tend to make us uncomfortable and to make our lives a struggle rather than a celebration. Of course, each person has to confront his or her own tyrants, but I would like to share with you now several distorted attitudes which I have found at the center of my own discomfort. I am sure that I have not yet made the new, corrective Christian attitudes completely habitual as yet, but I'm working on it. Also, I hope that my sharing will prime the pump of your own attitudinal inspection and revision. Remember: Only after we have discovered and revised our distorted attitudes will we be free to live the full and peaceful life to which our Lord calls us.

DISTORTED ATTITUDE #1: Being overresponsible. For a long time I saw myself as responsible for helping everyone who came to me in need. After I recognized this attitude and tendency, I slowly learned to laugh a bit at my delusion. I playfully called it my "Messianic Complex." While suffering from this attitude, I could not say "no" without a guilty feeling that I had turned away from someone in his or her hour of need. This overresponsible attitude also led me to believe that I had to have an answer for everyone who had a question. I had to provide a solution for everyone who had a problem. As you might well imagine, and as I know from experience, the overresponsible person becomes a tense and driven person. He frequently experiences emotional frustration and weariness. More and more he tends to relate to others only as a "helper." He allows others to lean on his strength while remaining weak in themselves. He cultivates a clientele of people who need him. His nerves are a bit frayed at times, but he feels good about all the people who could not possibly survive without him.

The new attitude I am cultivating: I am only one very limited person who has just two hands and twenty-four hours a day. If I am to stay sane and healthy, I need time to relax and enjoy, to think and to pray. It is better to refer people in need to others rather than to play at being a savior of all humankind and do a poor job. Also, problem-solvers almost always fall into the trap of becoming "enablers." They enable others to remain weak and immature. Enablers do for others what others could do for themselves. Enablers do not challenge others to grow stronger by working out their own problems. It is, of course, more loving to challenge others to grow by finding their own answers than to provide those answers ready-made. The truth is: "Give people a fish and they can eat for a day. Teach them to fish and they can eat for a lifetime."

been said that it is often easier to act yourself into a new way of ...ng than to think yourself into a new way of acting. When we begin to act on a new insight, the hardest steps are the first ones. As I began acting on this insight into my own overresponsibility, I found the tendency gradually leaving me, as though the monkey was slowly being lifted off my back. I began to act more like a fellow pilgrim than a mini-messiah. Admittedly, it was very difficult at first because changing a habit is always hardest in the beginning. However, I soon noticed that the world didn't stop, and no one died because I resigned my messiahship. The best part: I found out that I was more peaceful and that I was helping others to realize their own strengths and to use their own resources more effectively.

DISTORTED ATTITUDE #2: Being intolerant of conflicting positions and opinions. For a long time I harbored and practiced the attitude that it was essential that everyone agree with me, at least on issues which I regarded as important. The truths that I held as fundamental to belief in God and to human decency were, as I saw things, never to be challenged. Being outspoken, I often entered into conflict and heated arguments. The results were almost always unfortunate: Others remained unconvinced and I always felt drained by the conflict and emotionally upset in the wake of arguments.

The new attitude I am cultivating: Formerly I saw myself as the bold defender of absolute truth. I am now trying to accustom myself to a new set of lenses through which to see such matters. I am trying to recognize and to realize the relativity of truth: There are different ways of looking at the same truth, just as there are different sides from which to view a statue. Formerly I thought it was a part of my loyalty to my own convictions to speak up always, without compromise and without exception. I was not so determined to listen. I felt obliged to set the matter straight. Now at last I am learning that a win-lose debate almost always alienates others. Such debates seem to lock both parties deeper into their fixed and rigid positions. I also discovered that others will listen to me only to the extent that I am willing to listen to them. Again, by putting this new insight into practice, I am learning a new way of thinking. I am learning that empathic listening leads to a deep and rewarding sharing. And sharing is the essence of true human communication, which in turn is the heart of all human relationships. Finally, if I really do have a part of the truth that is worth sharing, the chances of success at communicating it are greatly increased by such an empathic sharing. A win-lose debate rarely has this happy outcome.

DISTORTED ATTITUDE #3: Taking myself too seriously. I just can't think of any other way to say it: I simply and for a long time took myself too seriously. Someone once said, and I can identify with the one who first said it: "I know of no man who has given me more trouble than myself." I also heartily endorse the new beatitude: Blessed are they who can laugh at themselves; they shall never cease to be entertained.

Looking through the lenses of my former attitude, I thought that everything I attempted, every speech I delivered, every class I taught, and all the words I spoke were vitally important because they would be carved in stone and remembered forever. I had to be good, stimulating, insightful, intelligent, and convincing because there was so much at stake. The very course and flow of human history would forever be affected by the pebbles I threw into its stream. Consequently, I felt dejected by failure, saddened by the apparent or real rejection of my person and/or my ideas. I was frustrated even by partial success because partial success always seemed to imply partial failure. The very Kingdom of God seemed to hang in the balance, to depend on me and my efforts.

The new attitude I am cultivating: As a Christian I must try to realize that God's strength comes through my human weakness. Saint Paul himself writes:

> But to keep me from being puffed up with pride because of the many wonderful things I saw [his mystical visions], I was given a painful physical ailment, which acts as Satan's messenger to beat me and keep me from being proud. Three times I prayed to the Lord about this and asked him to take it away. But his answer was: "My grace is all you need, for my power is greatest when you are weak." I am most happy, then, to be proud of my weaknesses, in order to feel the protection of Christ's power over me. . . . For when I am weak, then I am strong.
> *2 Corinthians 12:7-10 (GNB)*

God's Kingdom has historically been built on failures as well as successes. I remember some years ago studying the prophecy of Jeremiah, who never really succeeded at anything. The poignancy of his repeated failures is deepened by the fact that he didn't want to be a prophet in the first place. At one point, Jeremiah buries his face in his hands and moans:

> Woe is me, my mother, for you have borne me
> to be a man of strife and of dissension for all the land.
> I neither lend nor borrow,
> yet all of them curse me.
> Truthfully, Yahweh, have I not done my best to serve you,
> interceded with you for my enemy
> in the time of his disaster, his distress?
> You know I have! . . .
>
> Why is my suffering continual,
> my wound incurable, refusing to be healed?
> Do you mean to be for me a deceptive stream
> with inconstant waters?
> *Jeremiah 15:10-11, 18 (Jerusalem Bible)*

Somehow I think that Jeremiah, good and holy though he was, might have missed an important point. God can call us to what seems to be failure. God can build his own successes out of our failures. Certainly

23

Jeremiah and his prophecy have helped millions of people about whom Jeremiah could never have dreamed. And God can purify us and our motivation by allowing us the frustration of failure, at least as we humans judge success and failure. I would think that Christians are called to do their reasonable best in any attempt and then leave the results to God.

I see myself as needing an attitude that has a wide-angle lens. I need to take the "longer and larger view." I have taken myself too seriously because I have held the picture up too close to my face. I have lost perspective. I have to back away, in moments of prayer and reflection, to realize that God's strength operates through my weakness, that God writes straight with my crooked lines.

Mother Teresa of Calcutta, who has given her life to the destitute and derelict of India, was once asked, "How do you measure the success of your work?" The saintly, aged woman looked puzzled for a while, and then responded, "I don't remember that the Lord ever spoke of success. He spoke only of faithfulness in loving. The Lord has called me to faithfulness in love. This is the only success that really counts." Ultimately, it is this faithfulness that is the only real measure of our success as Christians. We are worth only what we are worth in God's eyes, no more, no less.

Summary

God calls us to the fullness of life. A deep, personal peace is the promise and legacy of Jesus to his followers. When the fullness of life and personal peace are interrupted by discomfort, whether it be physical or emotional or behavioral, the experience of discomfort is an invitation to personal introspection and reflection. What is in me? is the necessary and sometimes painful question that must be asked. I cannot change others, the world about me, the weather, or the position of my stars. I can change myself. In reflection and prayer, I can trace my discomfort to its attitudinal roots. I can look clearly at what is in me. And this is the area of my attitudes which I can control and change. There may be times when my attitude is found to be in full harmony with my Christian faith. But most of the time, if you are like me, you will find a neurotic and un-Christian attitude at the source of your discomfort.

And so I have to ask myself about alternative attitudes. I have to go out to others in my need, to explore the mind and attitudes of another who does not seem to be afflicted with my discomfort. It may also help to record in a journal a written description both of the old attitude to be unlearned and the new attitude to be acquired.

Have you ever felt that you were standing with another at an important fork in the road of that other person's life? If so, you probably sensed that if the person chose the less traveled road, it would make all the difference. I have that same feeling about this question we have been discussing. Each of us stands, I think, at the fork of a road in life. I can take the road of blaming: the other people in my life, the "way I am," the situation in which I find myself, the weather, the stars, and so forth. This road of assigning responsibility for my reactions to others is a dead-end road. At its end there is only death: the death of my growth and development as a Christian, the death of peace, the death of what might have been.

I have a sense that we can also choose the road marked, "What's in me?" Of course, there are some zigs and zags, some bumps and sharp turns in that road. There will be mountains to be climbed, waters to be crossed. Along that road we may feel very burdened at times with the tasks that honesty imposes upon us. But if we choose that road, we will eventually become whole by becoming profoundly Christian. We will be brand-new beings, new creations. We will become more like the Christ of our faith. And we will experience his peace, and possess the fullness of life that Jesus has promised as his gift and legacy to believers.

CHAPTER 3

Jesus: Metanoia
and the Master Vision

Jesus spoke to the Pharisees again. "I am the light of the world," he said. "Whoever follows me will have the light of life and will never walk in darkness. . . . If you obey my teaching, you are really my disciples; you will know the truth, and the truth will set you free. . . . If the Son sets you free, then you will be really free."　　　　John 8:12, 31, 36 (GNB)

John the Baptist: Metanoia

The forerunner and herald of Jesus was his cousin, John the Baptist. John, you will remember, stood waist deep in the waters of the Jordan preaching *metanoia* (conversion) to the people of Israel. John invited his people to come down into the waters of the Jordan for a ritual ablution or washing which would signify and symbolize the internal reality of *metanoia,* for all the world to see. *Metanoia* is often translated to imply a moral conversion, but the basic meaning of this Greek word, as well as the basic meaning of conversion, is "a change in one's outlook or way of thinking, a change of mind." John was calling for a change in the attitudes that governed the lives of his people. Immersion in the Jordan was only an external symbol of this inner change.

> So John appeared in the desert, baptizing and preaching. "Turn away from your sins and be baptized," he told the people, "and God will forgive your sins." Many people from the province of Judea and the city of Jerusalem went out to hear John. They confessed their sins, and he baptized them in the Jordan River.　　　　Mark 1:4-5 (GNB)

The Jews of John's time longed for the coming of the Messiah. They carried in their hearts a tremendous sense of personal dignity as God's chosen and covenanted people. Yet in the long course of their history, they were repeatedly humiliated by the political and military powers of other nations and peoples. At the time of John and Jesus, the Jews were chafing under Roman rule and a particularly cruel Roman prefect, Pontius Pilate. Most of them, I suppose, really wanted a political and military Messiah, who would forcibly break open their shackles and free them from their Roman tyrants. According to the way they were seeing things, this was the only practical solution to their problems.

In calling for a *metanoia,* a change of attitudes, John was in effect saying something like this to them:

27

I know what kind of Messiah you want. You want a Messiah with blood in his eyes and flames snorting from his nostrils. You want a political, military Messiah with a sword in his hand. But God is going to send us not a lion but a lamb, a lamb whose blood will save us. God is going to send us a Messiah who is meek and humble of heart. God's Messiah will ask us to turn the other cheek, to walk the undemanded mile, to love our enemies. In fact, God's Messiah will recognize only one power in this world: the power of love.

It is so hard for most of us to let another be other, be different from us. Something in us wants everyone to march to our drums, to believe in our beliefs, to honor our values, and to fight for our causes. John's call for a *metanoia* was a call to his people to let God be God, to let God save them in his way and in his time. "Be still," God had said to his people, "and know that I am God. . . . My thoughts are not your thoughts; my ways are not your ways." (See Psalm 46:10; Isaiah 55:8.)

"When you feel you can manage this surrender to God's higher wisdom and God's master vision," John was saying, "come down into the water. Conversion is an interior reality, a change of mind, a change in the way we look at things. If you are willing to change, then let everyone see and celebrate your willingness in this symbolic baptism."

One day, as John was baptizing a line of those willing to give up their old attitudes to learn new ones, he looked into the face of the man next in line. It was the Lamb himself. It was the gentle-strong, soft-hard figure of Jesus. John tried to demur but Jesus insisted. So John immersed him in the symbolic waters of the Jordan and then cried out:

"This is the one I was talking about when I said, 'He comes after me, but he is greater than I am, because he existed before I was born.'"
John 1:15 (GNB)

The Twelve Apostles: The Challenge of Metanoia

Beginning his career as a rabbi or teacher at the customary and required age of thirty, Jesus began to recruit disciples. All rabbis of the time did this. However, twelve of those chosen by Jesus were called to special roles and invited into a special intimacy, to be his regular companions, to preach the good news to the people, and to cast out demons. (See Mark 3:14.)

Jesus would spend the greater part of his life during the next three years preparing these twelve men. The master vision would be gradually laid out before them in the person and teaching of Jesus. In his teaching the Lord often used a literary form that began, "Blessed [happy] are they who . . ." We call them *beatitudes* because the Latin word *beatus* means "happy." These beatitudes were and are the Jesus-formula for true happiness and a full life. They call for a profound surrender of faith. "Blessed [happy] is the person who puts his faith in me!" (See Luke 7:23.)

28

Many of the old attitudes of these twelve were challenged by these new beatitudes. In fact, it seemed that Jesus was telling them that their life-wagers had been misplaced. The things that they thought would make them happy, Jesus seemed to be saying, were empty illusions that could only disappoint them. Often, his teaching seemed to make almost impossible demands.

> "But I tell you who hear me: Love your enemies, do good to those who hate you, bless those who curse you, and pray for those who mistreat you. If anyone hits you on one cheek, let him hit the other one too; if someone takes your coat, let him have your shirt as well. Give to everyone who asks you for something, and when someone takes what is yours, do not ask for it back. Do for others just what you want them to do for you.
>
> "If you love only the people who love you, why should you receive a blessing? Even sinners love those who love them! And if you do good only to those who do good to you, why should you receive a blessing? Even sinners do that! And if you lend only to those from whom you hope to get it back, why should you receive a blessing? Even sinners lend to sinners, to get back the same amount! No! Love your enemies and do good to them; lend and expect nothing back. You will then have a great reward, and you will be sons of the Most High God."
>
> Luke 6:27-35 (GNB)

Once I thought that the Twelve Apostles were a bit slow, that they were missing the candlepower or intelligence to learn the lessons of their Master. I had counted seventeen places in the Gospels where Jesus asks them, "Are you yet without understanding?" In our present-day jargon, we would probably translate this, "You don't get it yet, do you?" I once thought these things, but not now. I now think that the real challenge of Jesus was not a matter of intelligence but ultimately a challenge to give up an old vision and to accept a new one. It was a matter of radical faith and profound trust.

The Apostles had their own ideas of what would make them happy. I suspect that their hopes were largely grounded in material things: a boat full of fish, a fleet of boats, a full stomach and a full purse. No doubt they had their own plans for security and happiness, some less realistic than others. But with a little luck, a calm sea, and a couple of good seasons, they would have it made. They would be able to set up their children and sit back with their pipes and sandals to enjoy a little luxury as the shadows of their lives lengthened. Then into their lives came Jesus, shattering their worldly hopes and restructuring their self-centered dreams.

What they needed but were so slow to achieve was in fact a *metanoia*. Somehow the compelling figure of Jesus was able to call them away from their boats and nets and from their thriving little businesses; but they did not leave their dreams, their plans, their formulas for happiness with any notable eagerness or alacrity. They had their own set of beatitudes which did not include loving your enemies, giving away your material possessions, walking undemanded miles, or turning the other cheek.

Andrew and John

The first two of these Apostles to encounter Jesus were Andrew and John. As young men, Andy and Johnny used part of their spare time to help John the Baptist at the Jordan. It had its moments, but both knew that they were looking for something more promising and rewarding than immersing those people who had or pretended to have a conversion. When Jesus walked by the scene at the Jordan one afternoon, John the Baptist's eyes followed the strong, erect figure intently. "John, Andrew," he called to them, "there he is, the Lamb of God. Go follow him." (See John 1:35-42.)

Docile if nothing else, they literally walked behind Jesus, who apparently noticed these two curious fellows silently following him at a short distance. (This John, who later wrote the fourth Gospel, tells this story in the first chapter of his Gospel. He says that it all began about three or four o'clock in the afternoon.) Finally, Jesus turned to the two and asked, "Can I help you? What is it you want?" Somehow I think that the two young men were caught off guard by this direct question. They probably looked at each other, each hoping the other would answer. Then, staring down at their sandals, they probably kicked a little sand and shrugged their shoulders. Finally because nothing else occurred to either, they asked, "Where do you live?" Jesus said simply, "Come and see." John tells us that they went with him and stayed from four o'clock in the afternoon until it was dark. After leaving him, both young men ran off to their brothers. Andrew announced excitedly to his older brother Simon, who also helped John the Baptist in his spare time, "Simon, no kidding, we have found the Messiah!" It is not hard to imagine the older brother giving young Andrew the patronizing look that says, "Kid, you've been wearing your headband too tight." But he went to see anyway, and his name and his life were changed forever by that encounter. Simon, the son of Jonah, became Peter the Rock.

Peter's Problem

The call of Peter by Jesus is narrated in the fifth chapter of Luke's Gospel. It is easy to imagine the scene. Peter becomes painfully aware of his own weaknesses in the embarrassing moment following the miraculous catch of fish. Jesus had been suggesting a good place for Peter to drop his nets, but Peter kept insisting that he knew these waters, and there were never any fish there. Finally, Peter does drop his nets at the suggested place only to humor Jesus. And wow! Astonished and embarrassed, Peter wrinkles up his face, shakes his head, and pleads with Jesus: "Go away from me, Lord! I am a sinful man!" (Luke 5:8, GNB)

Peter had not been open to the suggestion of Jesus about fishing. He thought he knew more than the others. Likewise, Peter was not ready to trade in his plans, dreams, and desires in a *metanoia* which would lead him to a completely different outlook. Peter was not yet ready for a new life of dedication and love, a completely different set of values and goals. Right to the end of the public life of Jesus, three years later, Peter would still be struggling with this new vision.

Poor Peter had his great moments, but there were always evident footprints around his mouth. In the sixteenth chapter of Matthew's Gospel, we find the memorable statement of Peter: "You are the Christ, the Messiah, the Son of the living God!" Jesus congratulates Peter for his apparent gift of faith. However, a few verses later Peter takes Jesus aside to put him straight about suffering. Peter was probably counseling Jesus to play it safe: "Don't get involved and you won't get hurt!" Jesus is firm and crisp in his rebuke to Peter: "Oh, Peter, you are looking at things merely from a human point of view. You are not seeing things from God's point of view." (See Matthew 16:16, 22-23.)

Right to the end of the earthly life of Jesus, Peter was still struggling with his *metanoia*. Peter might well have worn that sign around his neck: "Please be patient—God is not finished with me yet!" As mentioned, most of the three years of what we might call their "novitiate," Jesus spent alone with the Twelve Apostles. Jesus was constantly laying out before them the master vision, with its completely different set of values. "In my Kingdom," he kept insisting, "all authority must be a role of service. The only acceptable motive is love. The only real force in this world is the power of love. Like me, you are called to love and to serve, not to lord it over others." It was a difficult lesson for Peter to learn.

In the thirteenth chapter of John's Gospel, we read of another interaction between Jesus and Peter. At the Last Supper Jesus takes up a towel and a basin of water to wash the feet of the Apostles. It was a Jewish custom to treat honored guests in this way. As usual, Jesus is living out his own teaching. But poor old Simon Peter does it again! He protests, "Oh, no. You're not ever going to wash my feet!" Once more Jesus has to be firm and direct. In effect, he says, "Peter, if you don't see that we are called to serve and that love is the only acceptable motive in the Kingdom of God, then you haven't understood me. And, Peter, if you don't understand me, you can't be my partner in the Kingdom." The good, if impetuous, instincts of Peter take over and he blurts out, "Lord, do not wash only my feet, then! Wash my hands and head, too!" (John 13:9, GNB)

Simon Peter, the Rock, very often looked more like a sandpile than a rock. But if I may be presumptuous enough to try a little post-mortem psychoanalysis, I feel sure that his real problem was not a lack of goodwill. I think that Peter had great goodwill and a very generous heart. But he did have a torturous time in giving up his own misconceptions, in surrendering his own way of seeing things. His *metanoia* was not noteworthy for its swift completion. Fortunately for him and for all of us like him, the patient Lord Jesus understood, and never gave up on his reluctant Apostle.

James and John: The Mama's Boys

Let's go back for a minute now, and start again at the Jordan. Like Andrew, John also had an older brother, James. Eventually Jesus called both of these brothers to the company of his twelve traveling companions, to be his disciples and eventually his Apostles. It is thought that James and John were "rich kids." Their father, Zebedee, who was probably known by some prestigious and flattering nickname like "Big Zeb," may well have owned a fleet of boats. The Aristotle Onassis of the Sea of Galilee. Zebedee was apparently a man of means because the Gospels tell us that he had servants and evidently through his wife, Salome, financed some of the preaching tours of Jesus and the Apostles. (See Mark 1:20; 15:40; Luke 8:2-3.)

At any rate, it is Salome, the mother of James and John, who comes to Jesus with arched eyebrows, saucer eyes, and an innocent little request for a political favor.

> Then the wife of Zebedee came to Jesus with her two sons, bowed before him, and asked him for a favor. "What do you want?" Jesus asked her. She answered, "Promise that these two sons of mine will sit at your right and your left when you are King." "You don't know what you are asking for," Jesus answered the sons. "Can you drink the cup of suffering that I am about to drink?" "We can," they answered. "You will indeed drink from my cup," Jesus told them, "but I do not have the right to choose who will sit at my right and my left. These places belong to those for whom my Father has prepared them."
> When the other ten disciples heard about this, they became angry with the two brothers. So Jesus called them all together and said, "You know that the rulers of the heathen have power over them, and the leaders have complete authority. This, however, is not the way it shall be among you. If one of you wants to be great, he must be the servant of the rest."   Matthew 20:20-26 (GNB)

With James and John, as with Andrew and Simon Peter, the problem again was *metanoia*. They seemed almost stubbornly to resist this change of vision. They were so reluctant to give up their old distorted, dead-end dreams about an earthly kingdom, where there would be thrones and genuflecting servants. A new vision did not come easily to the Apostles because, like so many of us, they had been practicing and protecting a radically different vision for years. Like the Rock, Jimmy and Johnny required much patience and understanding. I would be willing to bet that Jesus must have been smiling as he referred to James and John by their collective nickname, "The Sons of Thunder."

The story behind the nickname, it is thought, is this. James and John had protested to Jesus that they could take it, that they could drink from his cup. "Bring on the chalice of suffering!" However, on one occasion when Jesus and the Apostles were on the road, Jesus had sent some of them ahead to seek accommodations for all in a Samaritan village. The fact that Jews and Samaritans were not very friendly is well known. In fact, they did not even speak to each other. Recall the conversation that Jesus had with the woman at the well who asked him, "How is it that you, a Jew, are speaking to me, a Samaritan lady?" (See John 4:9.) At any rate, the word came back to Jesus and the Apostles that the Samaritan village wanted no part of them and would offer them absolutely no hospitality. "Jews need not apply!" This antagonism between Samaritans and Jews was eight hundred years old and was festered by political and religious as well as ethnic differences. The Jews used to call the Samaritans "half-breeds," and when the Jews really got angry at Jesus, they could think of no name to call him worse than "a Samaritan and a devil!" (See John 8:48.)

Faced with this resolute refusal of hospitality, Jimmy and Johnny have an immediate adolescent suggestion: "Call down fire (lightning and thunder) from heaven and burn the place up!" (See Luke 9:54.) The Gospel says only that "Jesus reprimanded them," but Jesus must certainly have been wondering how long it would take the Apostles to accept his vision and to absorb his values. I have often thought that if I had been Jesus, about halfway through the three years of public life, I would have called all twelve together and made an announcement: "Fellas, it's just not working out. I think maybe you should be doing something with your hands rather than with your heads." Sadly, however, the poor Apostles also seemed to be inept at fishing. In the Gospels the only fish they are recorded as catching were caught at the direction of Jesus and against their own protestations: "There are no fish there!" (See Luke 5:5.)

The Death of Jesus: Still No Signs of a Metanoia

Jimmy and Johnny were like Andy and the Rock. Jesus was calling them to a *metanoia,* a change of mind, a new vision; but it wasn't easy. In fact, the change was painfully slow in coming and was not in clear evidence until Pentecost. When the tides of public opinion ran out on Jesus, so did the Apostles.

When Jesus was arrested and tried before the Jewish Sanhedrin, during the trial Peter waited outside in the courtyard of the High Priest, Caiaphas. Just as he had once advised Jesus to do, he was "playing it safe." If Jesus asserted the miraculous power which Peter knew was tingling in his fingertips, then Peter would step forward and identify himself as "The Rock, Top Executive of the Apostolic College." On the other hand, if Jesus went on being the Lamb of God, well . . . Peter was just warming his hands over the fire in the courtyard. "That's no crime, is it?"

Then he was recognized. Perhaps it was his northern accent, his clothes, or more likely his face. But when he was challenged, Peter protested vigorously that he didn't even know Jesus. When others claimed to remember him as a disciple of Jesus, Peter resorted to an oath: "I swear before God that I don't even know him!" These words were hanging on the evening air as Jesus was being led out of the High Priest's palace. The eyes of Jesus and Peter locked into a dialogue of silent sadness and guilt. The awful words, "I don't even know who he is!" echoed between them. There must have been sadness in the face of Jesus, and shame in the downcast eyes of Peter. According to the gospel story, Peter "went out and cried his heart out."

> The Lord turned around and looked straight at Peter, and Peter remembered that the Lord had said to him, "Before the rooster crows tonight, you will say three times that you do not know me." Peter went out and wept bitterly. *Luke 22:61-62 (GNB)*

As he hung dying on the cross, the eyes of Jesus must have searched the jeering crowd below for the faces of his beloved friends, the Apostles. He had given his trust and love to these men. He was now giving his very life for them. However, as the arms of Jesus were stretched out as if to embrace the whole sinful world in the act of his dying, the Apostles were huddled and hiding in the upper room, with the doors barred and bolted. They were very visible public figures on Palm Sunday, but they faded fast into a safe obscurity on Good Friday. Jesus would have to die alone. The old way of seeing things, characterized by self-centeredness and self-protectiveness, was still the fixed mind-set of the Apostles. They seemed to be what we might call "fair-weather friends." But Jesus is committed to loving them into human wholeness and the fullness of life.

The Resurrection and a Reflection

And so Jesus comes to the Apostles on Easter Sunday morning to share with them his triumph over death. He tries to put them at ease with kindness and patient understanding. "Shalom!" he says. "Be at peace." The frightened Apostles are apoplectic. "We are seeing a ghost! We must be suffering from mass hallucination." The predictions of his resurrection, which Jesus had made previously, had been lost on them. So Jesus graciously offers to eat their fish and honeycomb, which ghosts don't ordinarily do. He patiently lets them touch him by way of reassurance.

> While the two were telling them this, suddenly the Lord himself stood among them and said to them, "Peace be with you." They were terrified, thinking that they were seeing a ghost. But he said to them, "Why are you alarmed? Why are these doubts coming up in your minds? Look at my hands and my feet, and see that it is I myself. Feel me, and you will know, for a ghost doesn't have flesh and bones, as you can see I have." He said this and showed them his hands and his

feet. They still could not believe, they were so full of joy and wonder; so he asked them, "Do you have anything here to eat?" They gave him a piece of cooked fish, which he took and ate in their presence.

Luke 24:36-43 (GNB)

The Apostles must have been deeply moved by this faithful act of love on the part of Jesus. They had been walking out on him and here he was, walking after them. It may well have been this act of kindness that broke down the barriers of their resistance. A few verses later (Luke 24:45) it is reported that Jesus "opened their minds . . ." The old vision was finally beginning to give way to the new, life-giving, joyful vision. It seems that making the vision of Jesus one's own is never really a completed process. Somehow I am sure that to the end of their lives, the Apostles, like Jesus himself, grew in wisdom, age, and grace.

The French author Leon Bloy once wrote that "the only really happy people are the saints. It is a pity *(tristesse)* that we are not all saints." The saints have put on the mind of Christ; to a great extent they have made his vision their own. They have experienced that peace which is the legacy of Jesus, that peace which the world can never give nor the human mind ever fathom. They have broken out of the strong shackles of a self-centered, self-protecting, self-seeking life vision. They have found that "fullness of life" to which Jesus invites all of us.

Why were the Apostles so slow to respond? Why are you and I, who are so much like the Apostles, so reluctant to give up our old way of seeing things in order to take as our own the vision of Jesus? It seems to be very much the same with all of us. We know the vision that we have, and we know what life is like with our present vision. We are not sure what would happen to us if we were to give up our old vision. Where would Jesus lead us? What would he ask of us? Perhaps deep down inside of us we are not yet ready to believe that walking undemanded miles and living a life of love will really make us happy. Perhaps we still prefer our beatitudes to those of Jesus.

Jesus and His Contemporaries: "The Comfort Zone"

In the eighth chapter of John's Gospel, Jesus is discussing this very point with his contemporaries. He is telling them that they are not free, and they are insisting that he is wrong. Jesus tells them that they are not free because their real tyrants are not outside but rather inside them. They are enslaved by the attitudes that rule their feelings, relationships, actions, and reactions.

"You are truly my disciples if you love the vision which I am offering you. Then you will know the truth, and the truth will set you free!" "But we are descendants of Abraham," they said, "and have never been slaves of any man on earth! What do you mean 'set free'?"

John 8:31-33

Jesus briefly explains to them again that their tyrants are not outside but inside them in their old crippling, distorted attitudes. He repeats, "If the Son of Man sets you free, you will indeed be free!" (John 8:36)

There is something very possessive about what has been called a "comfort zone." The Apostles experienced it. You and I experience this possessiveness. Only the saints seem to be able to break out of their comfort zones and find true freedom of spirit in the Lord Jesus. Psychologists tell us, and our human experience confirms, that we all tend to live in these comfort zones. We dress in certain comfortable ways, we live by a certain comfortable lifestyle, we think and plan with certain outside, comfortable limits. We are reluctant to step out of these comfort zones, to take risks, to try the new because . . . well, because we want to be comfortable. Stretching isn't comfortable.

If someone challenges me to give a speech before a large public audience or to be very open about my deepest and truest feelings, or asks me to swim against the tides of public opinion, I may well cop out by saying simply, "Oh, I can't. I just can't. I'm simply not the type. No, that's not me!" Defending myself with all these bromides, I stay where I am, huddled snugly in the warm corner of my comfort zone, playing it safe, staying out of the way of challenge and conflict. I thus remain forever shackled by the tyrants of fear, inferiority, and guilt. Before I can truly be set free by Jesus and his vision, there is a kind of open-handed surrender that must first be made, a willingness to break with my old postures and mind-sets.

I keep thinking of the Apostles and of many of the saints who struggled to preserve a crippling and withering vision before their surrender to the Lord. It was the great Augustine who, in his moment of surrender, reminisced about the thirty years of his resistance: "Memory is indeed a sad privilege. . . . Our hearts were made for you, O God, and they shall not rest until they rest in you. . . . Too late, too late, O Lord, have I loved you."

It is so difficult for us to give up our own plans, dreams, and formulas for happiness. It is so difficult to get out of the driver's seat and offer it to the Lord. It takes so much faith to leave our comfort zones and journey into the unknown. Of course, the less traveled road of faith could and would make all the difference. But a haunting sense of risk and a dread of the unknown tend to drown out the voice of grace inviting and challenging us. Our only guarantee is the word of Jesus: "If you follow me, you will not walk in darkness."

A Nearsighted Young Man

I once knew a young man who was born seriously myopic. He could see clearly only those objects within a few feet of himself. When the schools he attended sent this word home, his parents reasoned, "When we were his age, we did not need glasses. Why should he?" And so the boy grew up in the only world that was available to him through his nearsighted vision. He actually worked out an explanation for this world in terms of his nearsightedness. For example, do you know why the teachers at school write on the chalkboards? They are not writing for the pupils who cannot possibly read what they are writing. They are rather writing those notes on the board for themselves, so that they can remember what to teach. And do you know why cities put street signs so high up on telephone poles where no one can read them? Well, this is done for the bus drivers. They sit high up in the front of the buses and can read those signs. Then they can call out the names of the streets for their passengers. And so on.

One day the young man, in his eighteenth year, consulted an eye doctor. The doctor sat him down and kept experimenting with corrective lenses until he had the proper prescription. The doctor then told the boy to look out the window. "Wow!" the young man gasped. It was so beautiful. He could for the first time see the blue skies with white puffs of clouds. He could see the smiling faces of people, the billboards, and the street signs. Later he told me, "It was the second most beautiful experience of my whole life." So naturally I had to ask him about "the most beautiful." What was it?

"The day," he replied, "I came to believe in Jesus. When I at last took him seriously and saw that God is truly my Father, when I saw that this really is God's beautiful world, when I saw myself as a child of the heart of God, and felt the warmth of his love, when I saw others as my brothers and sisters in the human family of our Father—this was the great turning point, the most transforming and beautiful experience of my whole life. It was like the beginning of a new life. I know what Saint Paul means when he says that faith makes us a brand-new creation."

Metanoia: A Work of Grace in Us

I think that there are many critical realizations about this *metanoia*, this radical change of outlook. However, one realization seems to me to be the most fundamental. It is that *metanoia* is a faith experience and consequently the work of grace. Only God can make a person a believer, and only by believing in Jesus can we take on this vision. Faith is not and never has been a matter of intelligence or logical ability. If faith were a matter of intelligence, all people with superior intelligence and logical ability would become believers. In a sense faith is rather for the open-minded and the brave-hearted. Faith is for those gamblers who are willing to wager everything on Jesus.

God gives us his Word summarized in the Scriptures. Historically he tells us of his love in his communication through the patriarchs and the prophets of the Old Testament. Finally, in the course of human history, God breaks what sometimes seems like an eternal silence. God's Word becomes flesh and dwells among us. In Jesus, God offers us his supreme act and invitation of love. "God was in Jesus," Saint Paul says, "reconciling the world to himself," taking our world and all of us back into his arms. (See 2 Corinthians 5:19.)

However, all of this may well seem like a fairy tale, a magical myth, a melodrama without any real meaning, except for the grace of faith. Without grace it is fiction; with grace it becomes a fact. God's Word becomes real to us only when God touches us by his grace, empowering us to believe. When Peter said so forthrightly in Caesarea Philippi, "You are the Christ, the Messiah, the Son of the Living God" (Matthew 16:16), Jesus was quick to congratulate him, not for his intuitive genius but rather because God had obviously been very good to him. God had blessed him with a grace of faith. God had touched this man deep within his soul. And this is the first and most fundamental realization about the *metanoia* of faith: It is God's gift. It becomes ours only because we have experienced the touch of God. It is not a matter of intelligence but rather a matter of the experience of grace.

> "Good for you, Simon, son of John!" answered Jesus. "For this truth did not come to you from any human being, but it was given to you directly by my Father in heaven." *Matthew 16:17 (GNB)*

Jesus himself said, "No one can come to me unless the Father who sent me draws him to me. . . ." (John 6:44, GNB), and so Saint Paul could write to the church at Ephesus:

> For it is by God's grace that you have been saved through faith. It is not the result of your own efforts, but God's gift, so that no one can boast about it. *Ephesians 2:8-9 (GNB)*

Metanoia: A True Understanding of God's Word

There is a second central and critical realization about this change of vision called *metanoia*. If the *metanoia* of faith comes about when we really accept the Word of God on faith, it is very important that the Word of God be presented accurately. It is very important that it not be misrepresented to the prospective believer. If God's good news is misrepresented as a burdensome, frightening, and dehumanizing message, God cannot confirm this message with the grace of faith. If the message of faith were so misrepresented and God gave the grace of confirmation to this error, then God would be misleading us. This is unthinkable. And so Saint Paul insists that "we do not falsify the Word of God." And Paul also tells us in his letter to the Galatians (2:2) that he went up to Jerusalem to confer with the other Apostles, because he wanted to make sure that he was not distorting the good news.

A Spanish priest, Juan Arias, has written a very popular book entitled *The God I Don't Believe In*. Later we will quote this book at greater length. For now I would like to summarize what Father Arias says about God and his good news, which has been misrepresented in much of Christian preaching.

No, I shall never believe in: the God who condemns material things
. . . the God who loves pain . . . the God who flashes a red light against
human joy . . . the God who always demands 100 percent in examinations . . . the God who does not accept a seat at our human festivities
. . . the God who does not have the generosity of the sun, which warms
everything it touches . . . No, I shall never believe in such a God.[1]

And so it seems to me to be a matter of the greatest importance
that the Word of God be presented intact, as an announcement
of good news. This does not insure, of course, that all who hear
the Word will accept it and become the "new creations" of which Saint
Paul speaks. But it is certain that there can be no real *metanoia* of faith,
no new creation, unless the joyful and loving Word of God is presented
as such.

When anyone is joined to Christ, he is a new being; the old is gone,
the new has come. All this is done by God, who through Christ
changed us from enemies into his friends and gave us the task of making
others his friends also. Our message is that God was making all man-
kind his friends through Christ. God did not keep an account of their
sins, and he has given us the message which tells how he makes them
his friends. *2 Corinthians 5:17-19 (GNB)*

The Word of God Is Good News

It is clear that one must make prior assumptions before interpreting
the Scriptures. One's interpretation of the Bible will depend on his or
her assumptions. For example, we must make some kind of assumption
in this mattter: Does God really interact with us, responding to our peti-
tions and questions? Or does he pretty much leave us on our own? Some
Scripture scholars have opted for different assumptions in this matter.
Those who, like myself, believe that God does interact with us, would in
general interpret the inspiration of and the communications to the
Christians of the early Church as authentic and true. We would believe
that God did, through his Spirit, touch and direct these men and women.
However, those who make the opposite assumption would rather attach
a figurative meaning to the narratives about the early Church. Our conclusions, then, very much depend on our assumptions.

The assumption that I am making and trying to underline here is this:
The Word of God, when truly and faithfully presented, should sound
like good news to the hearer. The Word of God is basically an act of love
for us by the great and loving God who so magnificently strung the stars
in the sky, who built the mountains and filled the oceans. In his Word
this magnificent and almighty God is saying to each of us, I truly
love you.

---

[1]Juan Arias, *The God I Don't Believe In* (St. Meinrad, Ind.: Abbey Press, 1973), pp. 196-99.

If a mother were to forget the child of her womb, I would never forget you!   *Isaiah 49:15*

I have loved you with an eternal love.   *Jeremiah 31:3*

I have carved your name in the palms of my hands so I would never forget you.   *Isaiah 49:16*

Whoever touches you touches the apple of my eye.   *Zechariah 2:8*

Our Inability to Hear God's Good News

I think that one reason many of us do not really take into the marrow of our bones this message of the unconditional love of God is this: We dwell excessively on ourselves and on our mistakes. And so we keep asking, Who am I that the Lord should love me? Instead we ought to be asking, Who are you, O my God, that you love me so much? The Lord knows and accepts that we humans are mistake-makers. This is the human condition. Still, there is something in us that, with Simon Peter, keeps protesting, "Don't even come near me, Lord God. I am a sinful person. I am sure that you wouldn't want me around you." (See Luke 5:8.)

The Word of God reminds us that God sent his own Son into this world not to condemn us but rather to love us out of our selfishness and into the fullness of life. (See John 3:16-17.) The Word of God assures us that Jesus comes as an ambassador from the Father, as a Divine Physician precisely because we are broken, twisted, and sick. Jesus comes as the Good Shepherd precisely because we do go astray. He comes looking for us because he wants us with him, because he wants to take us into his arms and to celebrate the joy of finding us and having us once again close to himself.

Many of us wonder if we haven't put too much distance between ourselves and the love of God. We wonder if the warm rays of his love can still reach us. The Word of God reminds us of the parable Jesus used to explain how God feels about us when we have left him, left him in pursuit of our own dreams and plans, confident in our own formulas for happiness. We read in the Word of God the well-known Parable of the Prodigal Son. In this parable the Word of God depicts God's love and goodness as a constant. God is ready to embrace and to welcome us whenever we are ready to say "yes," whenever we are open and willing to be loved. God's patient love doesn't really care where we have been or what we have done. He is forever holding out wide and loving arms waiting to embrace us. The invitation is always the same: Come to me! Still there is something in most of us that keeps asking the wrong question: How could you ever love me?

Once a study was made of people who had given up faith in God. The reasons of these various people for giving up their faith were cataloged. Some ceased to believe because they felt churchgoers were "a bunch of hypocrites." I have always been personally unmoved by this reason. I always feel the impulse to say, "Oh, come on in. There's always room for one more hypocrite." However, the one reason that struck me as truly profound was this: "Faith did not *ask* too much; it *promised* too much. It was not that God's Word was too *hard* to believe; it was rather that it was too *good* to believe. Could a God of infinite power and majesty really lean out of heaven to take me in his arms, to claim me as his child, the child of his heart and the apple of his eye? I don't think so. It is just too much." The Word of God which we accept in our act of faith is indeed very good news—not too difficult but almost too much.

There is a story about Groucho Marx and a priest. It seems that the priest was walking along a busy boulevard in Los Angeles when he thought he recognized the great comedian. He tentatively approached him: "Pardon me, but aren't you Groucho Marx?" "Yes, I am, Father," the comedian replied, raising and lowering his eyebrows while tipping his cigar in his trademark fashion. "Well," said the priest, "I just wanted to thank you for all the joy and laughter you have brought into this world." The comedian is said to have replied, "And I would like to thank you, Father, for all the joy and laughter you have taken out of this world."

I can't really be sure that this story is true, but I am sure that very often the Word of God is misrepresented as threatening, fearsome, vindictive, dehumanizing, and withering. Consequently, the God of such a Word comes across as an angry, fearsome, and vindictive God—the kind of God in whom Juan Arias and I do not believe. The distorted, misrepresented Word of God does not offer us the vision that invites us to come running into the arms of a loving Father. Rather it condemns us to cower and cringe and grovel in the dust. We are invited by such a vision to think of ourselves as sewers. It seems obvious to me that God could not confirm such a message with the grace of faith. Those who reject such a vision and such a God have rejected an error, not a truth. The fruits of such a faith and such a vision would not be peace and joy, but rather anxiety and depression.

And so, my assumption is this: Jesus came into our world so that we might have the fullness of life, so that his joy might be in us and our joy might be complete. (See John 10:10 and 15:11.) I assume also that the legacy of Jesus is peace, the peace that the world can never give and that the human mind can never fathom. (See John 14:27 and 16:33.) My own assumption would differ radically from that of those who see this life as a time for "mourning and weeping" and from those who see this world as a "vale of tears." Saint Augustine, who was far from a frivolous saint and certainly not an intellectual lightweight, once suggested that we should all be "an allelulia, from the top of our heads to the bottom of our feet." Even in those moments when I do not feel very much like an allelulia, I have a sense that this is because I am not really taking in the true Word of God. The problem is with my vision and my blindness of heart. Like the Apostles I am slow to grasp this vision of joy and peace, slow to accept the truth that will set me free. And so I pray, "Lord, I do believe. Help me with my unbelief." Like Bartimaeus, the blind man sitting outside the gates of the city, I also pray, "Lord Jesus, Son of David . . . that I might see." (See Mark 10:46-52.)

What is to Come

In the following pages I would like to describe this joy-filled and liberating master vision of Jesus, as I understand it. I know very well that our Christian understanding of Jesus, his message and vision, is progressive. Each generation stands on the shoulder of the previous generation. Like pigmies standing on the shoulders of giants, we of this generation should understand the person and vision of Jesus better than previous generations. And those Christians who will come after us should see more clearly than we do the meaning of his person and message.

I can only share with you, my sisters and brothers in Christ, the Jesus whom I know and his vision as best I can understand it at this time in my life and at this point of human history. I trust that there will be others who have more profound insights than I do. I trust that there will be others who will take up where I must leave off, who will see and understand the person and vision of Jesus more clearly than I do. However, I do want to share with you the insights that are helping me to become a more peaceful and a more fully alive believer. Of this one thing I am certain: To the extent that you and I truly understand and live the vision of Jesus, we will be that much more free to live, to love, to grow, and to experience the fullness of life that Jesus holds out to us.

CHAPTER 4

The Christian Vision of Self

> "My heart praises the Lord;
> my soul is glad because of God my Savior,
> for he has remembered me, his lowly servant!
> And from now on all people will call me happy,
> because of the great things the Mighty God
>   has done for me.
> His name is holy."   Luke 1:46-49 (GNB)

An Experiment: The Empty Chair

Before we explore the question about how we Christians are to think of ourselves, I would like to ask you to do another experiment. (By the way, thanks for your patience with me and my experiments.) I would like you to close your eyes after you have finished reading the instructions. Imagine a chair at a distance of about ten feet from yourself. Please notice the appearance of the chair: its height, width, color. Notice, too, the type of chair: straight back or rocker, upholstered or wood, and so forth. After the chair becomes very vivid to you in your imagination, let someone you know very well come out of the wings of the stage of your imagination and sit in the chair. Please look carefully at this person, and notice the way this person looks at you. You will then register a "felt sense" of the person. Become aware of your total, unified reaction to this person: physical (bodily), emotional, perceptual. All of your previous experiences with this person will feed into this "felt sense." All the things you have ever thought or judged about this person—your previous emotional reactions, your stored memories of past experiences with this person—will all shape and color and contribute to your reaction.

After you record this reaction, see the first person getting up and leaving. Then a second person whom you know very well comes and sits in the same chair. Again, you consciously record your "felt sense" of this second person. You can compare it with your previous reaction, the "felt sense" of the first person. After you have finished with the two persons, let a third person come from the wings of the stage and sit in the chair, face to face with you. This third person is yourself. Notice and become more and more aware of your "felt sense" of yourself. Notice and remember the immediate reaction you have to yourself: warm or cold, heavy or light, enjoyable or painful, a sense of attraction or revulsion, and so forth. The main thing is to record your "felt sense" reaction to all three persons, the last of whom is yourself. Please review these instructions and then put the book down for now. When you get back, I would like to make a few suggestions about the significance of the results of your experiment.

*　　*　　*

The exercise you just conducted was an effort to get at your "self-image." Imagining the other two people was just a warm-up, getting you used to the awareness of a "felt sense." The real test was the reaction to yourself which you experienced. Your thoughts and judgments, your feelings and memories of yourself all fed into and determined that reaction. Recall now: Did you like or dislike yourself? Did you feel warm and friendly, turned on or off by the image of yourself? What would you like to have said to yourself? What did the face and the body language of "the other you" seem to be saying to you?

I recall that the first time I did this experiment, the "me" that I saw looked tentative and uneasy, as though he was bracing himself for impending criticism. I instinctively felt very sorry for him. Suddenly it dawned on me that I have always been my own severest and constant critic. I have never been able to review my own personal performances. I can't watch myself on film or listen to myself on a recording. It has even been painful for me to read the words that I have written. The critic in me has always been commenting: "Why did you say that? Why didn't you use a different illustration? Your voice is high pitched and nasal! That idea does not come through clearly!" When I realized this, during the chair fantasy, I remember apologizing to myself: "Hey, I'm sorry. I have never really been an affirming friend to you. I have been only a negative critic. From now on I am going to try to be a friend, to notice and to tell you about your strengths as well as your weaknesses, about your gifts and your goodness as well as about your limitations and failures."

The Most Important Attitude and Its Effects

There is no doubt that the attitude each of us has toward himself or herself is the most important of all our attitudes. We have earlier compared an attitude to a lens of the mind. To continue with this comparison, the lens or the attitude one has toward self is *always* over the eyes of the mind. Other lenses or attitudes may be superimposed when we are reacting to something else, but this lens-vision of self will affect favorably or unfavorably the way we see everything else. Depending on what we are dealing with, our various attitudes are always ready to interpret, evaluate, dictate an appropriate response. However, it is important to realize that the attitude toward self is *always* in play, always affecting our other attitudes, always coloring the way we see every part of reality. It is, without a doubt, the basic or fundamental attitude in each and every one of us.

Perhaps the most critical function and result of this attitude toward self is this: Each of us acts out his or her self-image. For example, if I perceive myself as a loser, I act like a loser. I approach each new person or situation with a loser mentality. All my expectations are colored by this "loser" perception of myself. And, as we all know, the expectation is often the mother of the result. Our expectations of failure give birth to our actual failures. And when in fact we do lose or fail, we are then confirmed in our original self-defeating attitude. "You see, I told you I was no good! I failed again." It is indeed a vicious circle.

There is a story in American Indian folklore that illustrates this truth very clearly. According to the legend, an Indian brave came upon an eagle's egg which had somehow fallen unbroken from an eagle's nest. Unable to find the nest, the brave put the egg in the nest of a prairie chicken, where it was hatched by the brooding mother hen. The fledgling eagle, with its proverbial strong eyes, saw the world for the first time. Looking at the other prairie chickens, he did what they did. He cawed and scratched at the earth, pecked here and there for stray grains and husks, now and then rising in a flutter a few feet above the earth and then descending again. He accepted and imitated the daily routine of the earthbound prairie chickens. And he spent most of his life this way.

Then, as the story continues, one day an eagle flew over the brood of prairie chickens. The now aging eagle, who still thought he was a prairie chicken, looked up in awed admiration as the great bird soared through the skies. "What is that?" he gasped in astonishment. One of the old prairie chickens replied, "I have seen one before. That is the eagle, the proudest, the strongest, and the most magnificent of all the birds. But don't you ever dream that you could be like that. You're like the rest of us and we are prairie chickens." And so, shackled by this belief, the eagle lived and died thinking he was a prairie chicken.

So, too, does each of us live and die. Our lives are shaped by the way we perceive ourselves. The all-important attitudes by which we perceive and evaluate ourselves tell us who we are and describe the appropriate behavior for such a person. We live and we die according to our self-perception.

There is still another very important effect of the attitude toward self. This attitude determines not only how we will act but also how others will treat us. No doubt you remember the nasty kid in grammar school, who pinned a sign on your back which read: "Kick me!" (And other nasty kids obliged.) Well, it seems to be true that our attitudes toward ourselves, the way we perceive ourselves, compose a message or sign also. Only this sign that you and I hold out in front of ourselves is something like an announcement of who we are. It tells other people who we are and invites a definite reaction. Like the children at school, most people treat us accordingly. If my sign says that I'm not much, that's about how much attention, respect, and affirmation I will get: not much! On the other hand, if the sign composed by my attitude toward self says that I am a person who deserves respect, I will be treated with respect by others.

A postscript has to be added to what has just been said about this "sign" which is composed and held out in front of us, reflecting our attitudes toward ourselves. We may consciously try to pretend, to develop a public personality which belies what we truly think and feel about ourselves. We may try to camouflage our anxiety by an outward show of arrogance. We may pretend confidence when we are trembling inside. However, it really doesn't get us very far. Most people see through our transparent masks. We have a sense, don't we, that tells us when another is being "real" and when that person is striking a public pose. We want to ask the braggart, "Are you trying to convince us or yourself?"

Subconsciously, in a thousand ways that we might try to hide, we publicly reveal our self-images. We tell people, as clearly as if there were a visible sign held out for all to see, what we truly think about ourselves. And most people, reading our giveaway signs with instincts that are partly conscious and partly subconscious, treat us accordingly. Human intuition can be frighteningly accurate. People are much more perceptive than perhaps we realize. And so, when troubled people come to a counselor to ask how they can change the other people with whom they are dealing, the counselor almost always gives the same advice: "Change yourself. Change your own attitude toward yourself, and other people will automatically change in their treatment of you."

Love of Self and Love of Others

Finally, it is a fact that we cannot love others if we do not love ourselves. The commandment of the Lord is to love our neighbors as we love ourselves. A psychological version of this commandment might well read: "Love yourself and you will love your neighbor. Refuse to love yourself and you won't be able to love your neighbor." The Jesus I know insistently tells us to put away our pan scales, to stop measuring output versus input, to make love the rule and motive of our lives. "Love one another as I have loved you." Further, Jesus assures us, "If you do this, you will be very happy." (See John 13:17.) However, it is crucial to realize that our attitude toward self regulates our active capacity for loving others. The hard fact is that only to the extent that we love ourselves can we truly love others, God included.

If our attitude toward self is crippling, our capacity to love is proportionately diminished. The pain of a poor self-image is like the noisy strife of a civil war inside us. It magnetizes all our attention to ourselves and leaves us little freedom to go out to others. When we are hurting, even from a simple thing like a toothache, we have only a diminished availability for others. If our attitude toward self leaves us with an ache of emptiness, we have no strength or desire to go out to others. However, as our attitude toward self grows more positive and supportive, our pain is proportionately reduced and we are to that extent more free to read and respond to the needs of others around us. In short, the better the self-image, the larger the capacity for loving. On the contrary, the greater the distraction of pain, the smaller will be our capacity to love and care about others.

A memory from my own past convinces me of this truth. My career as a teacher was launched on a bright September morning in a boys' high school. We novice-teachers were instructed to be very businesslike, efficient, masterful, clear, inspiring, and spellbinding. We were warned that we should not smile until Christmas. Otherwise, those adolescent rascals would run away with us. On that bright September morning, I remember the butterflies in my stomach and the trembling hope that I would be able to remember my own name. During that whole first year of teaching, a real baptism by fire, the only question that preoccupied me was, How am I doing? My main interest in teaching well and in preserving an atmosphere of discipline was centered mainly on my own desire to succeed as a teacher. I was so busy reading and responding to the needs of my own insecurity that I had only a small capacity left over to read and respond to the needs of the young men whom I was teaching.

Gradually I realized that I was in fact a good and competent teacher. (Permit me a moment of immodesty, okay?) As I came more and more into the possession of self-confidence, my inner anxieties about personal success and my fear of failure abated. Proportionately my capacity to care about the needs and concerns of my students started growing. I felt myself moving slowly but certainly from the self-centered question, How am I doing? to the more loving question, How are you doing?

It is very much this same way with our attitude toward self. If we focus mainly on our limitations, if we remember vividly our failures and see in ourselves only doubtful value, we will be preoccupied with ourselves. We will always be asking the nervous question, How am I doing? The inner anxiety, the sense of inferiority, the fear of failure will leave very little freedom and availability to read and respond to the needs of others. However, as we slowly and certainly come to a healthier attitude toward self, we will find an increased capacity to care about those others whom Jesus has asked us to love.

My List of Likable Qualities

I am personally convinced that only by truly loving myself will I be able to love my neighbor and my God; and this love is my life ambition and my life-wager. And so, in balance with my efforts to fulfill the needs of others and contribute to the Kingdom of God, I consciously work at improving my self-image. My own deepest desire is, with grace of God, to make my life an act of love. And I know that this is the first and indispensable step: I must love myself. I must try to recognize and appreciate the unique gifts that God has given me. And so, I have made out an alphabetized list of everything I like about myself. (I alphabetized the list so I wouldn't repeat too often.) My list includes everything from the color of my eyes and my love of music to the deep, instinctual compassion that I feel for those who are suffering.

I keep this list in the center drawer of my desk for two reasons. The first is that it is close at hand for reading when I tend to get down on myself. It is also easily available when I discover a new likable quality in myself. The second reason is a bit more facetious. I tell others that I keep this list in the center drawer of my desk in the event of my own sudden death. It will furnish some ideas for the person who is assigned to write my obituary. The presence of this list in my desk also provides for another contingency. When others come to see me and seem to be suffering from problems that arise because of a crippling attitude toward self, I suggest that they write out such a list. When they express astonishment or disbelief, exclaiming that I cannot be serious about this, I show and let them read my list. (P.S. There are currently about three hundred entries on my list!)

Also, when people offer me a compliment, my own tendency is semihumorously to ask them "to expand on that," because it will help me to increase my self-appreciation and my gratitude to God, who has been so good to me. The bottom line is this: My only chance to love you and God is based on my ability to appreciate and love myself. And so I work at it. Loving ourselves is our only chance for a happy life. Furthermore, if a person truly loves himself or herself, not much can make that person seriously unhappy. Such a person will have a built-in insulation against harsh and unkind criticism. Such a person can truly accept and enjoy being loved by others. In addition to all this, if I truly love myself, I am with someone I like twenty-four hours a day.

On the other hand, if I do not love myself, not much can or will make me happy. I will feel crushed by criticism because I will secretly believe that I deserve it. I will not be able to take in compliments or truly accept the offer of love from others because I will reason, "If you really knew me, you would not love me." If people insist on loving me, I will question their motives and wonder about their angles. The dark shadows and distortions of a crippling attitude toward self, the way I perceive myself, will discolor and distort everything else I see. To me it is obvious that a healthy attitude of self-appreciation is essential for a peaceful soul and a happy life.

The Danger of Conceit or Pride

At this point we might ask, Can a person love himself or herself too much? I would like to suggest that the answer, with one important qualification, is most probably "No!" Self-centeredness is not the result of self-love, but the product of pain, the result of a poor self-image. A self-centered person has a toothache—an ache of emptiness inside. This poor person attempts to fill the aching emptiness with bragging, name dropping, posing as an authority on all questions great and small. What may look like an excess of self-love in fact represents an absence of self-love. Erich Fromm rightly maintains that selfishness and true love of self are at opposite ends of the spectrum. One does not suddenly slip over from true self-appreciation into the trap of selfishness. In fact, the greater the self-appreciation, the less danger there is of selfishness.

There is one important qualification to which I have already alluded. What I am about to say represents a relatively recent insight for me. For a long time it seemed to me that there was some opposition between love of self and the Christian virtue of humility. My former understanding of humility required a person to deny resolutely anything good about self, and to focus all one's conscious attention on personal faults and failings. I sensed, even while doing this, that it was a course of psychological self-destruction.

So I was delighted to find that one of the Fathers of the Church, Saint Ambrose, Bishop of Milan in the late fourth century, had a very different idea of humility. He proposed that the "perfect expression of humility" is found in the Magnificat of Mary, the mother of Jesus.

According to the Gospels, the setting was this: Mary's cousin, Elizabeth, was about to give birth (to John the Baptist). It was a Jewish custom that all women relatives should come to such an expectant mother, at the time of her delivery, to offer their help. I suspect that besides wanting to help, Mary was also anxious to share the secret of her womb with her cousin. At any rate, shortly after the announcement of the angel to her, Mary sets off on the seventy-five-mile journey from Nazareth to Ain Karim, a southwestern suburb of Jerusalem. When Mary arrives, Elizabeth is surprised: "Why should such an honor come to me, that the mother of my Lord should come to visit me?" Mary, we might well imagine, falls into the warm embrace of her cousin and explains:

> "My soul magnifies the Lord, and my spirit rejoices in God, my Savior. For he has smiled upon me, his little servant girl, and now all generations will call me 'blessed' because he, the mighty and holy one, has done such great things in me. Holy is his name." Luke 1:46-49

Saint Ambrose found in these words the perfect expression of humility. The virtue of humility first of all implies a grateful appreciation of all God's gifts. Second, it involves an acknowledgment that all these gifts of God are pure gifts. None of us has any claim on God. All of his gifts to us are totally the result of his goodness and not in any way the result of our worthiness. God has smiled down upon his servants and has endowed each of us with such unique gifts that anyone who truly knows us will know that we are indeed "blessed" by our Father. If we did not appreciate our unique gifts, we would certainly be failing in gratitude to our good and generous God.

Once a wise old teacher was speaking to a group of young and eager students. He gave them the assignment to go out and find by the side of some lonely road a small, unnoticed flower. He asked them to study the flower for a long time. "Get a magnifying glass and study the delicate veins in the leaves, and notice the nuances and shades of color. Turn the leaf slowly and observe its symmetry. And remember: this flower might have gone unnoticed and unappreciated if you had not found and admired it." When the class returned, after carrying out the assignment, the wise old teacher observed: "People are like that. Each one is different, carefully crafted, uniquely endowed. But . . . you have to spend time with them to know this. So many people go unnoticed and unappreciated because no one has ever taken time with them and admired their uniqueness." In a true sense, each one of us is a unique masterpiece of God.

The One and Only You

Obviously—and I hope this suggestion is not misconstrued as an exercise in narcissism—the place and the person with whom to begin is oneself. Carl Jung says that we all know what Jesus said about the way we treat the least of his children. But then Jung asks, "What if you were to discover that the least of the children of God is . . . *you?*" If you were judged only on how well you have appreciated and loved yourself, the least of his children, would you get a glowing and affirmative judgment?

Most of us have a constant struggle with a sense of inferiority. We tend to play a painful comparison game. "So and so is smarter than I . . . This other person is stronger, more beautiful, or more athletic than I . . . That other person over there is more musical, although I am richer and have more clothes . . . ," and so forth. It goes on endlessly, and each new person we meet offers a new contest of comparison.

True appreciation of our personal uniqueness offers each of us the truth that sets us free from these endless and painful contests. God says to each of us: "You are unique, the one and only you. From all eternity and into all eternity, there will be only one you. I have loved you with an eternal love. I do not get new ideas nor do I lose old ones; so the thought of you has always been in my mind. And the image of you has always had a special, warm place in my heart. You have been given an important role to play in my world. You have a unique message to deliver, a unique song to sing, a unique act of love to bestow. This message, this song, and this act of love have been entrusted exclusively to the one and only you."

The Word of God assures us:

> There were many other possible worlds I could have created. Yes, I could have made a world without you. But, don't you realize this, that I

didn't want a world without you? A world without you would have been incomplete for me. You are the child of my heart, the delight of my thoughts, the apple of my eye. Of course, I could have made you different: taller, shorter, born of different parents, born in a different place and into a different culture, endowed with a different set of gifts. But I didn't want a *different* you. It is *this* you that I love. Just as every grain of sand on the seashore and every snowflake that falls in wintertime has its own unique composition and structure, so are you composed and structured as no other human being has ever been. It is *this* you that I love, that I have always loved and will always love. If you should ever get down on yourself and feel that you are the type that only a mother could love, please remember this: "Even if a mother should forget the child of her womb, I will never forget you!"

Seeing Oneself Through the Eyes of a Critic

One final thought about the attitude toward self. Though most of us are publicly defensive when criticized by another, privately we are usually our own worst critics. Earlier I mentioned *The Fully Alive Experience*, prepared and presented by Loretta Brady and myself. This seminar was comprised of four basic steps: (1) an explanation of how attitudes interpret and evaluate our experiences, determine all our actions and reactions, and consequently shape our lives; (2) an explanation of how to locate the distorted or crippling attitudes that may be keeping us from the experience of peace and joy and life in all its fullness; (3) suggested methods to change these distorted, crippling attitudes into healthy and life-giving attitudes; (4) an investigation of the basic, most fundamental human attitudes, including the attitude toward self.

One year after we had given our seminar in a large midwestern city, I received a letter from one of the participants. I would like to share this excerpt:

> Your seminar advertised for "emotionally stable people in search of further growth." Well, I sneaked in. I have always been a psychological basket-case, complete with frequent hospitalizations, suicide attempts, and the continuous care of a psychiatrist. I knew, however, as I left the Fully Alive Experience, that I was cured, that my troubles were at last ended. A month later, by mutual agreement, I terminated with my psychiatrist. I have not needed his help for a full year now.
>
> The transforming, healing insight was this: I had always viewed myself through the eyes of a critic. I was constantly reproaching myself, scolding myself for failing, being disappointed in the way I looked, regretful about the things that I did. I kept a careful log of all my mistakes both by commission and omission. I always saw myself through the lenses of a relentless and heartless critic. The juror in the court of my mind was forever finding me "guilty on all counts."

I saw clearly that my attitude toward myself was utterly destructive. In the wake of this insight, for the first time I felt truly sorry for myself. The compassion I had extended only to others I finally extended to myself. Of course I don't want to wallow in the swamps of self-pity. But I did promise myself that in the future I would try to be a true friend, that I would look for the gifts more than for the limitations, for the beauty more than for the ugliness, for the goodness in me more than for my regrets.

I didn't write to you immediately to tell you about this for fear that it was an emotional high that would quickly vanish like a cruel mirage. Since a year has elapsed now I feel safe in sharing this with you. I have indeed been healed. I am not only functional but alive. I am happy and free at last. Thank God!

At a subsequent Fully Alive weekend, one of the participants admitted to me: "I have to tell you that I did not come to this weekend primarily for myself. I just wanted to find out what happened to my friend [the author of the letter just quoted]. Believe me, my friend is now a changed person: optimistic, full of energy, in love with life."

You and I can profitably ask ourselves: What do I see when I look through the lens of my attitude toward myself? Am I more a critic or a friend? Do I look beyond the surface blemishes to find the truly beautiful and unique person that I am? Or do I play the destructive "comparison game"? What verdict does the juror of my mind pass on me: "good at heart" or "guilty on all counts"?

The Intolerable Burden of Perfectionism: "Be Perfect . . ."

I remember what a great and endless consolation it was for me to find out that the often used quotation, "Be perfect as your heavenly Father is perfect" (Matthew 5:48), is really a mistranslation. The context of this quotation is the challenge of Jesus to love our enemies. The Lord points out that we must try to be worthy children of a heavenly Father, who "causes his sun to rise on bad men as well as good, and his rain to fall on the honest and the dishonest alike." The challenge he extends is not to be perfect, which is impossible for us mistake-makers, but to be as tolerant and loving and forgiving as our heavenly Father is!

I remember sitting with this scriptural passage and with this insight for a long time, breathing great sighs of relief that God was not really asking the impossible (perfection). It was as though a very heavy burden had been lifted from my shoulders. I suddenly realized that God was not challenging me to be perfect but to be patient, to be tolerant and understanding of weakness, in others and especially in myself. I felt sure that Jesus was asking me not for perfection but for presence, to share my life with him, much as married couples promise each other in their wedding vows. Jesus was not insisting on instant or even ultimate perfection. He was inviting me into a covenant much like marriage. Married couples equivalently say to each other, "We have and we will experience the human condition of weakness. We will inevitably fail each other at times. But we are going to make it *together.*" It is something very much like this that the Lord asks of us and that we Christians promise to him in our faith commitment: "We are going to make it . . . *together!*"

A healthy Christian attitude toward self acknowledges and accepts the human condition of fragility. But we always see ourselves walking through life hand in hand with the Lord, feeling glad to be who we are, knowing that he accepts and loves us as we are. Our Father who is mighty has indeed done great and beautiful things in us and for us, and holy is his name. Only through the lenses of this vision can we find the peace and the joy which are the legacy of Jesus. Only if we see ourselves in this way can we experience the fullness of life which he came to bring us.

CHAPTER 5

The Christian Vision of Others

> When the Pharisees heard that Jesus had silenced the Sadducees, they came together, and one of them, a teacher of the Law, tried to trap him with a question. "Teacher," he asked, "which is the greatest commandment in the Law?" Jesus answered, "'Love the Lord your God with all your heart, with all your soul, and with all your mind.' This is the greatest and the most important commandment. The second most important commandment is like it: 'Love your neighbor as you love yourself.'"
>
> Matthew 22:34-39 (GNB)

People Are Basically ... What?

Occasionally I visit a prisoner in the State Penitentiary of Illinois. I certainly don't think it would be a good idea to free all such prisoners, but I do find it emotionally difficult to see human beings locked in cages. As you may know, more than ninety percent of all the prisoners in our American prisons have been abused as children. In the language of Transactional Analysis, they think of themselves as "not O.K.," but they also think that "you're not O.K. either." The vindictive, Papillon mentality is strong in them: "You hurt me and you're going to pay for it through your clean, blue nose!" The more violent prisoners are transported wearing thick leather girdles, to which are attached strong steel handcuffs. Most of those whom I have seen were sneering, defiant, and contemptuous of the beefy trustees who were leading them around.

On the occasion of one such visit, I was being processed as a visitor (translated: questioned, searched, x-rayed, and registered on a written form). Next to me was an elderly black woman who was visiting her grandson. She was so warmly gracious and kind to everyone around her that I could not resist the comment: "I have to say this to you. You seem to live what I preach. You come across as a very loving person, and I'll bet you bring a lot of joy into this world." She smiled and thanked me. Then she added, "Father, I am a Christian. In my world there are no strangers, just brothers and sisters. Some of them I have not yet met." All of my instincts recognized the presence of this beautiful attitude in her bearing and manner. "You really believe that, don't you?" I said. She replied simply and softly, "Yes, I do." On the other hand, the prisoner whom I visit has a very different attitude toward humanity. He tells me in detail about the subhuman conduct of many of the prisoners and of his general distrust of others. His motto seems to be "Don't trust anyone, and always carry an 'equalizer.'"

If the attitude toward self is the most important one of all those that reside in your head and mine, no doubt our second most important attitude is the way we view others. Of course, whenever someone speaks of an attitude toward others, we immediately want to distinguish: "Some people I like, others I don't. Some people are nice, others aren't." Still there is in us a general instinct about other people. There is a general anticipation: People are basically ___(what?)___ until they prove otherwise. What would your juror-attitude in charge of evaluating others fill into that blank? People are basically "good . . . bad . . . selfish . . . loving . . . cruel . . . kind . . . honest . . . deceitful . . . domineering . . . afraid . . . manipulative . . . generous . . ." and so forth. Pick one or more but let your choices come spontaneously out of your guts and heart rather than out of the stock of memorized answers in your head. Respond out of your *real,* rather than out of your *ideal,* self.

I would like to share with you that in my own efforts at introspection and investigation of personal attitudes, this attitude toward others seems to be the one attitude in me that is most in need of work and revision. I envy people like the elderly lady at the state prison. When I grow up, I want to turn out like her. I want to think of others as my brothers and sisters, even the ones I have not yet met.

Just as you must be, I am also aware of the extremes in this matter. Some of us are rosy-cheeked, naive, and gullible. We don't seem to acknowledge the effects of original sin. Others of us tend to be sour-faced and cynical. We are sure, as we see others through our suspicious and squinting eyes, that everyone is "rotten to the core." These are the extremes. Most of us stumble around somewhere in between them, looking for a middle ground.

The Source of Our Attitude Toward Others

The first, inherited attitudes of children are usually taken in by osmosis from their parents. When we were little kids playing with our toy cars or dolls, we heard our parents talking about others. We heard them talking about the people with whom they worked and the people in the neighborhood. Their messages, expressed and implied, were recorded on our "parent-tapes." These parent-tapes tend to play insistently, however softly, in our heads, for the rest of our lives. If there are certain messages on these tapes which we judge to be unhealthy, we must make a conscious effort to delete them.

In addition to this parental source of our attitudes toward others, there is also the dimension of personal experience. A frightening bully in the schoolyard, the ridicule of our elementary school classmates, a traumatic deception by a supposed friend, an attack or abuse suffered as a child—such experiences can plant seeds of distrust and suspicion in us that do not die easily. All of us have some unpleasant experiences with others which are stored in our memory banks.

One's personal psychological development also has a profound influence on his or her view of others. In the normal course of human growth, the first stage of child development involves an *attachment* or *dependency*. The child becomes deeply attached to his or her mother (primarily) so that she is the indispensable source of security, comfort, and reassurance. After this period, the child usually turns to its father for *guidance*. The child at this stage needs and seeks the approval of its father, and fears his disapproval and rejection. Then comes the period of *separation,* in which the young person leaves the protection and direction of parents, and becomes his or her own mother and father. In the first stages, the parents provide roots for their children. In the last stage, the parents must assist their children by offering them wings, the wings on which they can leave the nest of security and venture forth into their own independent lives.

If a person does not successfully negotiate these broadly outlined transitions, he or she can spend the greater part of life looking for the missing pieces. Such a person can easily become overdependent on the approval and reassurance of others, or can remain indecisive, hitchhiking through life on the judgments and decisions of others. Some people remain bottomless wells in need of reassurance by others or perpetually intimidated by a supposed inferiority to others. In any case, our attitude toward others usually has deep roots in the soil of our early lives. As mentioned, the abused child comes into later life angry and filled with vendettas of vengeance. Those who come from close, affirming, and affectionate families will come into later life, fully equipped with roots and wings, ready to bless and be blessed by others. "Our lives are shaped by those who love us . . . and by those who refuse to love us."

The Master Vision of Others

In the master vision, provided by the message, life, and person of Jesus, we Christians are called to be channels of love to one another. God, who is love, created us in an act of love. All goodness is somehow self-diffusive. In the act of creation God's goodness diffused itself. We all know what this diffusion of goodness means from personal experience. When we have something good—like a good joke, a good recipe, or even a bit of good news—the instinct of love is to share it. So our Father-God, experiencing in himself an ecstasy of love and happiness, wanted to share his life, his happiness, and even his home with us. From all eternity he planned this and picked out each of us to be the special recipients of his love. We are the chosen children of his family and of his heart. Each of us was conceived and born into this world only because we were loved and wanted by our Father-God.

From the beginning there was a human network of veins and arteries through which this love was to be carried to all the parts of God's human family. However, somewhere, somehow, something went wrong. We call it "original sin." Sin and selfishness, hatred and homicide became a part of our human inheritance. But the call has always remained the same.

> Jesus answered, " 'Love the Lord your God with all your heart, with all your soul, and with all your mind.' This is the greatest and the most important commandment. The second most important commandment is like it: 'Love your neighbor as you love yourself.' The whole Law of Moses and the teachings of the prophets depend on these two commandments." *Matthew 22:37-40 (GNB)*

In the Christian vision these two commandments are really linked together. I cannot say my "yes" of love to God unless I say my "yes" of love to each and every member of God's human family. There are to be no exceptions. The French poet Charles Peguy once said that if we try to come to God alone, he will certainly ask us some embarrassing questions: "Where are your brothers and sisters? Didn't you bring them with you? You didn't come alone, did you?" These yeses of love, required by the two great commandments, are inseparable. Jesus himself made this very clear: We can refuse our love to no one.

> "You have heard that it was said, 'Love your friends, hate your enemies.' But now I tell you: love your enemies and pray for those who persecute you, so that you may become the sons [and daughters] of your Father in heaven. For he makes his sun to shine on bad and good people alike, and gives rain to those who do good and to those who do evil. Why should God reward you if you love only the people who love you? Even the tax collectors do that! And if you speak only to your friends, have you done anything out of the ordinary? Even the pagans do that!" *Matthew 5:43-47 (GNB)*

"Aye!" as Shakespeare once said, "there's the rub!" The two yeses of love are inseparable. In fact, Jesus never talks about loving God without adding the second part of the great commandment, namely, a love of neighbor. Also, with the exception of the great commandment itself, Jesus does not even talk explicitly about loving God. He does say that God takes as done to himself whatever we do to the least of his children. He also instructs us that we should not offer God our gifts unless and until we have been reconciled with one another. (See Matthew 5:23-26.) Finally, Jesus insists that we cannot expect God's forgiveness for our sins unless we stand ready to forgive those who have offended us. (See Matthew 6:12.) In the message and master vision of Jesus, the principal place of encounter with God is in others: our families, friends, neighbors, acquaintances, and yes, even our enemies.

There is an old Irish ditty: "To live above with the saints we love, ah! that is the purest glory; but to live below with the saints we know, ah! that is another story." Let's face it, some people (not you or I, of course) are hard to live with, let alone love. Those who are truly loving and caring people must see something in others that I do not.

Two Persons in Each of Us

For myself, I think that my Christian commitment asks me to love others for themselves and not in spite of themselves. So I would suggest that there really is a vision that enables us to love people who are apparently unlovable. It seems to me that there are really two different persons in ourselves and in each of the others whom we meet. There is a wounded, hurt, and angry person: the obnoxious person. Wearing various outward appearances, it may be that this person is usually in the ascendancy in the personalities of the unlovable. This wounded, hurt, and angry person can be called out of any of us by harsh criticism, by sarcasm, by ridicule, and by put-downs. But there is also in each of us a good and decent, a caring and loving person. We are made in the image and likeness of God, and this likeness is never totally obliterated. This beautiful and loving person is called out by gentle kindness, by love and understanding.

As a newly ordained priest I volunteered to preach a week-long retreat to other priests. I felt confident at the time I accepted the invitation: "Have sermons, will travel!" But at zero hour, standing outside the chapel, watching my retreatants file past me into the chapel, I was completely intimidated. There were two bishops, and the youngest of the priest retreatants looked about fifteen years older than I. Through my saucer eyes, every single one of them looked completely confident, utterly together, and worthy of the most respectful veneration. At the time I accepted the invitation, I thought I had it all together, but when the chips were down I was wondering where I had put it.

The older priest in charge of the retreat house was standing with me at the chapel door. We were reviewing the troops together. He smiled at me as the last priest retreatant went into the chapel.

"How do you feel?" he asked.

"Terrified!" was my spontaneous and utterly honest reply.

"Why?"

"Why? You're kidding. Didn't you see them?"

"Oh, they just need what every one of us needs, a little love and a little understanding."

"Then why don't they look like it? Those fellas didn't look like they were lining up for love and understanding. Are you sure that's what they need?"

"I'm sure," he said with a knowing smile and friendly wink.

So began the retreat. During the first conference my mouth was dry and my hands were cold and clammy. Between the lines of their facial expressions I read this question: "Where did we get this kid?" I swore I could hear them thinking, "Sonny, the oils of ordination are not yet dry on your hands. When you have been over the ropes of life for a few more miles, come back and we will hear you again."

At the end of the first conference I just knew I should have volunteered for the foreign missions rather than arrogantly assume the task of preaching to my elders. However, even on that first day of the retreat, the priest retreatants began coming in to consult me. I couldn't believe it! They were so good, so humble, and some of them seemed to be hurting rather badly. One elderly, white-haired priest poured out his troubled soul to me like a small child talking confidently to his father. I remember thinking, "I hope that when I am your age I have half the humility, knowledge of self, and openness that you do." By the end of the retreat, I knew the truth beyond all doubt.

It is true and will always be true: We are all in need of a little love and a little understanding. And it is this love and this understanding that will draw out of us all the goodness and giftedness with which each of us has been blessed by God our Father. And it is probably also true that even we ourselves cannot know the depths of our own goodness and giftedness until someone else first loves us and calls these things out of us. The following simple lines of verse have been attributed to Roy Croft.

> I love you,
> Not only for what you are,
> But for what I am
> When I am with you.
>
> I love you,
> Not only for what
> You have made of yourself,
> But for what
> You are making of me.
>
> I love you
> For the part of me
> That you bring out;
> I love you
> For putting your hand
> Into my heaped-up heart
> And passing over
> All the foolish, weak things
> That you can't help
> Dimly seeing there,
> And for drawing out
> Into the light
> All the beautiful belongings
> That no one else had looked
> Quite far enough to find.

I love you because you
Are helping me to make
Of the lumber of my life
Not a tavern
But a temple;
Out of the works
Of my every day
Not a reproach
But a song.

I love you
Because you have done
More than any creed
Could have done
To make me good,
And more than any fate
Could have done
To make me happy.

Jesus: His Understanding and Love

I am convinced that this is how Jesus once loved the people of his time. I am convinced that this is how Jesus today loves you and me. It is this understanding love, which is not blind but rather supersighted because it sees beyond appearances, that the Lord commends to us when he proposes, "Love one another as I have loved you." (John 13:34)

Jesus calls the buried goodness and giftedness out of the depths of people. Just as surely as he called Lazarus, four days dead, out of his grave, so Jesus, by loving them, called the outcasts and the estranged, the lonely and the defeated back into the fullness of life.

Little Zacchaeus was a "runt" and up a tree in more ways than one. He was a physically small man who became the chief publican at Jericho, a rich tax collector who gouged and clawed his poverty-stricken fellow Jews and sent their taxes to the pompous emperor of Rome. Nobody liked him. You and I probably wouldn't have liked him. However, one day, as Jesus was moving slowly through the crowds that always followed him, Zacchaeus climbed up into the branches of a sycamore tree just to get a look at this Jesus. He never could have dreamed what was to follow. He was astonished to see Jesus making his way toward the very sycamore in whose branches he was perched.

Then Zacchaeus heard those unbelievable words: "Zacchaeus," Jesus was calling, "I'd like to stay here in Jericho tonight. Could I stay with you at your house?" Can you hear the thunder of excitement in the little man's heart? "He wants to stay with me!" (See Luke 19:1-10.) The crowd obviously didn't share the little publican's excited joy. The Gospel says only that they "started grumbling." Zacchaeus, we are told, jumped down from the tree, and in his great, excited joy pledged half his goods to the poor. Furthermore, he promised to restore fourfold whatever he had gained dishonestly. Jesus then reassures the little man that salvation had come to his house on this day, for the Son of Man had come looking "to seek and to save" those who are lost. The buried goodness and giftedness of Zacchaeus had surfaced at the touch of Jesus and his understanding love. Somehow I feel sure that the little man and his world were never the same again.

Then there was Mary of Magdala, which was a village on the west coast of the Sea of Galilee. She is frequently identified with the prostitute who bolted into the banquet at the house of Simon the Pharisee and wept at the feet of Jesus. However, there is no scriptural grounds for this identification. Nevertheless, according to Mark (16:9) and Luke (8:2), Jesus had cast seven demons out of this woman. Whatever her past, Mary Magdelene was really present and available to the needs of the Lord. Once the good and beautiful person was called forth by the understanding of Jesus, she loved boldly and recklessly. She stood bravely on Calvary as Jesus was dying (Matthew 27:56). She must have been taunted there by those who knew of her past, and ridiculed for her new religious posture and piety. "Hey, Mary, what's all this pious stuff? We all know who you really are!" However, I feel sure that she was far too strong to be much affected by the taunting.

It was Mary Magdalene who assisted at the burial of Jesus (Matthew 27:61). Again, it was Mary who discovered the empty tomb on Easter Day (Matthew 28:1-10). The importance of Mary Magdalene in the whole resurrection story is clear in the Gospel of John (20:1-18). She seems to have been the first to see the risen Jesus. Like Zacchaeus, the depths of strength and a fierce loyalty in loving had been called out of this great and strong woman by the love of Jesus. Zacchaeus and Mary of Magdala and countless others of us can truly say this to Jesus:

> I love you . . . for what you are making of me. I love you for the part of me that you bring out; I love you for . . . passing over all the foolish, weak things that you can't help dimly seeing there, and for drawing out into the light all the beautiful belongings that no one else had looked quite far enough to find.

The Beginning of Love: Empathy

It seems to me that the key to success in so seeing and loving others is empathy. Empathy starts with an attentive listening and an intuitive reading of the uniqueness of another. Empathy asks only one question: What is it like to be you? Empathy is getting inside the skin of another, walking in his or her shoes, seeing and experiencing reality as it looks through the eyes of another. In the end, empathy offers not advice but only understanding. "Oh, yes, I hear you." If the essence of empathy is listening to and living vicariously the life experience of another, the price of empathy is this: It requires a temporary leaving of one's self, one's own thoughts and feelings, one's values and beliefs. When I empathize with you, I leave where I am and I go to be with you where you are.

Carl Rogers suggests that our experience of the human condition often involves the feelings of a person who has fallen into a deep, dry well. The desperate man trapped in the well can't climb out, so he keeps knocking, knocking, knocking on the side of the well, hoping against hope that someone will hear him and realize his situation. Finally, after a long time of such banging against the side of the well, he hears a responding knock from the outside. Someone has heard him! There is an explosion of joyful relief in the poor man. "Thank God! Someone finally knows where I am." Rogers says that when someone really listens to us and registers understanding, we feel the same grateful explosion of relief: "Thank God! Someone finally knows where I am. Someone finally knows what it's like to be me!"

The experience of most people would seem to indicate that there are not many really good listeners among us. When we try to share who we are, many others tend to leap in, reduce us and our sharing to a problem, and proceed to solve the problem. They volunteer to tell us what to do. At other times they may seem to question the sincerity of our communication: "You don't really mean that, do you?" Or they go off into a narration of their own, assuring us that they have gone through our experiences in their own lives. None of these reactions is a part of empathic listening. I know you are really hearing me only when the expression of your face registers my present feelings, only when your voice and body language say, "So that's what it's like to be you . . . I hear you."

The empathic listener does not judge, criticize, or direct, because in the act of empathy we leave our own positions, our perceptions, and most of all our prejudices. Our concentration is given totally to the vicarious experience of another's person. We break our fixation with self by getting out of ourselves and into the other's thoughts, feelings, and life situation.

When we have identified with another in this way, we are already supplying the primary need of everyone: to have someone who really understands what it's like to be me! "All they need is a little understanding and a little love," the old priest said. Only after immersing ourselves in the experience of empathy can we know what we might say or do or be for another person's happiness and well-being. Loving is indeed an art. There are no automatic decisions or fixed and final formulas when we are trying to respond to the needs of another. We might have to be tough or tender, to talk or be silent, to sit at another's side or allow that person the luxury of aloneness. Only the empathic person can master this art.

The Two Essential Gifts of Love

Whatever else love may ask of us in a given case, there are two indispensable gifts that are always a part of loving. We can always be sure that these two gifts are needed. The first is the gift of self through self-disclosure. All the other gifts of love—like flowers, jewelry, cigars, and candy—are mere tokens and symbolic expressions. The essential gift of love is always the gift of myself. If I do not give you my true and authentic self, I have given you nothing. I have given you only pretense and sham. I have let you watch my charade.

The second essential gift of love is the affirmation of the other person's worth. If I am to love you, somehow I must appreciate and reflect back to you my appreciation of your unique goodness and giftedness. I cannot interact with you without making some contribution, either positive or negative, to your all-important self-image. Nor can I so interact with you without taking away some increase or decrease in my own sense of personal worth. We are all like mirrors to one another. We perceive ourselves largely in the "feedback" of one another's reactions. We are always contributing, positively or negatively, to one another's self-image. I can know that I am worthwhile only in the mirror of your smiling face, only in the warm sound of your voice, and in the gentle touch of your hand. And you can understand your worth only in my face, my voice, and my touch. "All they need is a little understanding and a little love!"

By way of summary, then, the eyes of love see in every other person not one but two persons: the wounded and angry, the good and gifted. It is understanding and love that call forth the good and gifted person. This is the way that Jesus loved people like Zacchaeus and Mary Magdalene and the Twelve Apostles into the fullness of life. The essential prelude to love is always empathy, which breaks our own self-centered fixation and provides for the other the inestimable good feeling of being understood. Having given a listening and available heart in empathy, we must go on to respond to the specific needs of those we love. The two specific needs we can be sure of are the gift of ourselves in self-disclosure and the gift of our affirmation of the other's worth.

At the beginning of this chapter, we filled in a response about people in general: People are basically __(what?)__ . One certain answer is: *needy*. No matter how much we try to conceal our need for understanding and love, we are all thirsty to be understood and hungry to be loved. Only when this thirst is quenched and this hunger filled can we be the fully alive people the Lord has called us to be. This is the way Jesus himself sees us and this is the way his master vision invites us to see one another.

CHAPTER 6

The Christian Vision
of the World

*God saw all he had made, and indeed it was
very good.* Genesis 1:31 (Jerusalem Bible)

Traditional World Rejection

After entering the seminary at the ripe old age of seventeen my classmates and I were given most of our instructions by a Master of Novices. Father Master solemnly informed us that we had been called "out of the world." We were assured that this was a blessing because the three major sources of temptation were "the world (usually listed in first place), the flesh, and the devil." Most of us novices were only teenagers, but we had ponderous discussions that sounded like those of aged veterans in an old people's home. We started many of our sentences with the sober, reflective introduction, "When I was in the world ..."

One of our novices had to have his eyes checked, so he boarded the bus from our rurally situated novitiate for the big city of Cincinnati. He asked the bus driver, "What is the fare now?" The driver responded politely, "Thirty-five cents." The surprised novice countered, "Gee, when I was in the world it was only a quarter." The bus driver looked at him quizzically and asked, "Fella, I don't mean to get personal, but where do you think you are?"

Somehow, almost from the beginning of Christianity there were some who left the so-called world, escaping to the dusty deserts and hidden places to avoid contamination and temptation. Everything, but especially material things like the human body (often called "the evil and ugly prison of the delicately beautiful soul"), was to be despised. These escapees from the world believed that Christians were obliged to crawl through a long, dark tunnel of detachment until they came to the beatific light at the end, which was found only in death. There are probably very few Christians who think this way today, but we still have remnants of this thinking in prayers that portray us as "sending up our sighs," and crying because we are the "poor banished children of Eve, mourning and weeping in this valley of tears, in this period of exile."

Incarnational Spirituality: To Seek and Find God in All Things

The attitude of world rejection seems to ignore the words of Genesis that "God saw all he had made, and indeed it was very good." World rejection ignores the theologically sound, incarnational spirituality that "seeks and finds God in all things." Ignatius of Loyola could not look at the stars in the night sky without being moved to tears by God's beauty. Teresa of Avila found the sweetness of God in the taste of grapes. Philip Neri's two favorite books were the New Testament and his *Book of Jokes.* Gerard Manley Hopkins, a Jesuit priest and poet, said that "the world is charged with the grandeur of God." Hopkins proclaimed that "Christ plays in ten thousand places" and that God should be glorified "for dappled things." "There lives the dearest freshness deep down things" because the Holy Spirit "over the bent world broods with warm breasts and with ah! bright wings."

So we must ask ourselves: How would a true Christian believer see this world? What is the liberating truth about this world with its many parts that I must know in order to be set free? If I truly "put on the mind of Christ," how would I perceive the world? If I could see through the eyes of Christ, what would the world look like? What attitude toward this world will free me to be a fully alive person for God's glory, to experience the peace and the joy that are the legacy of Jesus to his followers?

Definition of "The World"

Before attempting an answer to these questions, I would like to define what I mean by "the world." As I am using the term here, the world embraces all created reality, *except persons.* Consequently, the world in this usage would include all material things, but it would also include such immaterial things as personal talents and abilities, personal qualities and attainments. These are abstract terms, aren't they? Concretely, the list of created realities implied under "the world" would include such things as money, house, books, piano, typewriter, good looks, athletic ability, a charming smile, curly hair, straight white teeth, good health, academic degrees, artistic talent, a sense of humor, compassionate instincts, intellectual genius, love of nature, a reputation, power or influence, personal charm, and charisma. In our discussion, these are the types of things that I am including in the all-encompassing term "the world." All these things are part of my world. How am I, as a Christian believer, to regard them? If the gospel message were really in the marrow of my bones, if my mind and thoughts were drenched by the vision of Jesus, what would my attitude toward this world be?

The Spirits of Possession and Dispossession

As best I can understand Jesus and his good news, it seems that Christian spirituality involves both a spirit of possession and a spirit of dispossession. To be able to integrate and harmonize these two spirits is the genius of Christian spirituality. By possession I mean the ability to join God in his pronouncement over creation, "It is very good!" Possession would also include the ability to acquire knowledge of and to enjoy the good things of God's world, including one's own personal gifts and blessings. Possession reaches out to embrace life and all the parts of life. The glory of God is a person who is fully alive. The Christian spirit of possession sees a unique beauty in each of the seasons of the year, hears the music and poetry of the universe, smells the fragrance of a day in spring, and touches the soft petals of a flower. Possession tastes the deliciousness of every newborn day. Possession likewise includes experience of the whole galaxy of good feelings which are a part of our humanity: a sense of accomplishment when I have written a poem or have sung a song to the world, a feeling of appreciation when I am praised and thanked, a joy at being able to run fast or to tell a humorous story. In short, the spirit of possession tends to make me fully alive in my senses, emotions, mind, and will. The spirit of possession helps me become fully functioning in all the parts of my unique giftedness.

The genius of Christian spirituality is to integrate this spirit of possession with the spirit of dispossession. My possession of the world must be exercised in the spirit of readiness for dispossession. The spirit of dispossession implies that all these good and delightful things are never allowed to own, possess, or shackle me. Dispossession implies that I am always free, my own person, liberated from the tyranny that possessions can easily exercise over us. I always remain my own free person. The world may never dominate or manipulate me. The world may never be allowed to preempt my freedom to make my own decisions. All of us have some sense of what it is to be tyrannized, manipulated, or coerced by another human being. Things—even the good, delightful, God-made things of creation—can do the same to us. They can enslave us and deprive us of our freedom. What would it profit us if we should gain the whole world and suffer the loss of our own freedom, of our own persons? In a gospel parable, Jesus describes this tyranny of possessions.

> Jesus went on to say to them all: "Watch out and guard yourselves from every kind of greed; because a person's true life is not made up of the things he owns, no matter how rich he may be." Then Jesus told them this parable: "There was once a rich man who had land which bore good crops. He began to think to himself, 'I don't have a place to keep all my crops. What can I do? This is what I will do,' he told himself; 'I will tear down my barns and build bigger ones, where I will store the grain and all my other goods. Then I will say to myself, Lucky man!

You have all the good things you need for many years. Take life easy, eat, drink, and enjoy yourself!' But God said to him, 'You fool! This very night you will have to give up your life; then who will get all these things you have kept for yourself?' " And Jesus concluded, "This is how it is with those who pile up riches for themselves but are not rich in God's sight."
Luke 12:15-21 (GNB)

Clenched Fists and Open Hands

There is an old adage, "We are all born with clenched fists, but we must all die with open hands." I personally like this symbolism of clenched fists and open hands. These two expressions aptly symbolize the spirits of possession and dispossession in incarnational Christian spirituality. I reach out to take into my hands the fullness of life and creation. But nothing is ever so fastened into my grasp that I cannot give it up. Nothing is really enjoyable unless we are free to release it, to give it up. Without this freedom we are possessed by our possessions. We become the slaves of our own addictions. We are not masters but mastered. Our spirits are shackled and our souls are slowly shriveled. Recently I read a little story, a parable, that describes well what I am trying to say.

> He asked me what I was looking for.
> "Frankly," I said, "I'm looking for the Pearl of Great Price."
> He slipped his hand into his pocket, drew it out, AND GAVE IT TO ME. It was just like that! I was dumbfounded. Then I began to protest: "You don't want to give it to me. Don't you want to keep it for yourself? But . . ." I said.
> When I kept this up, he said finally, "Look, is it better to have the Pearl of Great Price, or to give it away?"
> Well, now I have it. I don't tell anyone. From some there would just be disbelief and ridicule . . . Others would be jealous, or someone might steal it. Yes, I do have it, but there's that question—"Is it better to have it, or to give it away?" How long will that question rob me of my joy?[1]

The Biblical Imperative: Love Persons and Use Things

The biblical imperative is quite clear: We must *love* persons and *use* things. Jesus warns us that wherever our treasures are, there will also be our hearts. As I hear him, the Lord is saying, "Save your heart for love, and give your love only to persons: to the persons of yourself, your neighbor, and your God. Don't ever give your heart away to a thing. If you do, that thing, whatever it might be, will gradually become your master. It will own you and will lead you around on the leash of addiction. Worry about it will keep you anxious and awake at night. But worst

---

[1]Theophane the Monk, *Tales of a Magic Monastery* (New York: Crossroad Publishing, 1981), p. 10.

of all, if you give your heart away to a thing, you will soon begin the great inversion of priorities. When you begin to *love things,* you start to *use persons* to get those things, to get more and more of those things. And so, we notice that the Bible does not say that money is the root of all evil, but rather that love of money is the root of all evil. Having money isn't an evil, but giving your heart away to money is a tragedy. Wherever your treasure is, there your heart will be. If you give your heart away to the things of this world, you will soon begin competing with others to get all you can. You will begin to burn the candle at both ends in order to acquire more and more. It is the wide and well-traveled road to high blood pressure and ulcers, to anxiety and depression. If you choose to run down this road, you will eventually be tempted to cheat, to swindle, and to compromise your integrity for a "fast buck" or a "big deal."

The Kingdom of God, which will be treated at length later on in this book, is an invitation on the part of God to be his, to belong to him in love. On our part, the Kingdom of God is a response of love, a "yes" to this invitation. However, it is critically important to notice that the invitation of God is not extended to us individually as individuals. We are called into the People of God, into a faith community of love. We are invited to become a part of God's family. By the very nature of the invitation we can come to God only together or we cannot come at all. This is the radical meaning of "Thy Kingdom come!" The bottom line is this: I cannot say my "yes" of responding love to God's invitation without saying a "yes" of love to you. It is impossible for me to love God and not to love you. Likewise it is impossible for you to love God without loving me. And so, as we have seen, Jesus tells us that if we come to place the gift of our love upon his altar, and we remember an unforgiving grudge, an estrangement from another, we should resolve that first. Only then are we invited to come and lay our gift of love upon God's altar. Jesus is very clear about this: We cannot love God without loving one another.

Sometimes, like a family squabbling over the material inheritance of a deceased relative, we are separated from this love of one another by the tyranny of things. You will remember the story of Jesus and the "rich young man." The poor fellow couldn't accept the invitation to follow Jesus in the Kingdom because of his attachment to his possessions.

> Jesus said to him, "There is still one more thing you need to do. Sell all you have and give the money to the poor, and you will have riches in heaven; then come and follow me." But when the man heard this, he became very sad, because he was very rich. Jesus saw that he was sad and said, "How hard it is for rich people to enter the Kingdom of God! It is much harder for a rich person to enter the Kingdom of God than for a camel to go through the eye of a needle."
>
> Luke 18:22-25 (GNB)

The Tyranny of "Loved" Possessions

As I hear him, Jesus is saying that the tyranny of possessions is a very real danger. "Blessed are the poor in spirit . . ." means that only those will be truly happy who are ready to open their hands in dispossession. Happy are those who give their hearts only to love and who will give their love only to persons. Sometimes it is difficult for us to hear this message, just as it was for the rich young man. But if we fail to free ourselves from these attachments and addictions, it will mean the gradual death of love for one another; and this is what the Kingdom of God is all about. When we begin to love things—whether they be material things such as money or immaterial things such as power, prestige, and status symbols—we will inevitably be trapped and enslaved. The people in our lives will soon begin to experience the sad truth: We do not really love them. Rather we love our "things." Our treasures and our hearts are elsewhere; they belong to our things.

I suspect that we have all experienced the difficulty of possessing without being possessed. When we got our first bicycle or car, the shiny new possession preoccupied our attention and concern. We were somehow diminished in our ability to think about the needs of others. Our availability to them and to their concerns was noticeably lessened. At the time, we could only think, "Heaven help anyone who puts a scratch on my bike or a dent in the fender of my car!"

I recall a story told to me by a young mother. It seems that she drove her children to the beach for a swim. When she finally got there in their ancient and balky family station wagon, the children eagerly flung open the doors, and one of the doors put a slight scratch on the BMW (Bavarian Motor Works = $40,000) in an adjoining parking space. The owner of the BMW, who was near his car, flew into an absolute rage, verbally scalding the children and abusing the young mother. "Do you know what this car costs?" he asked in a high-pitched scream. Finally, fearing for her own physical safety and the health of this poor outraged man, the young mother called a policeman, who had to look carefully before he finally found the almost indetectable scratch. The officer knitted his eyebrows and asked in puzzlement, "Is this what you are so excited about?" It is indeed difficult to be a rich man, to have many valuable possessions and still respond to the call and values of the Kingdom. Where our treasures are, there our hearts will be, and the hands which are clutching many valued possessions do not open easily. And the simple fact is this: Open hands are needed to enter the Kingdom of God.

I remember also an eighty-year-old millionaire telling me that he had slept only fitfully on the previous night. He explained that he himself wrote the radio commercials for his lucrative business, and it seems that he had tossed and turned his way through the dark hours of the previous night trying to think of a new commercial that would enrich him further. "The commercials," he observed, "bring in a lot of money, you know." I remember the heavy sadness I felt for this financially wealthy but personally impoverished old man. He had invested his heart in the currency of this world. He had deposited his soul in earthly banks. "Here you are," I thought, "worth many millions of dollars and you are near the end of your life. Still, you are losing sleep and turning your soul inside out in search of clever gimmicks that will make you even richer. You do not own your money, you poor old man; your money owns you."

The same kind of possessive addiction is possible, of course, with nonmaterial things: prestige, power, success, honor, reputation, public admiration, the pleasure of the senses, triumphs over and conquests of other people. I recall a televised interview with child movie star Jackie Cooper, now a sixtyish director. Cooper reflected that most of the child stars of his day had become seriously embittered adults. When asked to explain this pervasive bitterness, he suggested that these people had once been the center of attention. They once stood in center stage, in front of the footlights, and had been given star billing and all that goes with it. Now, as the shadows of their lives began to lengthen, they were deprived of these things. The glitter of their early careers had disappeared. People ask about them only in the questions of "old movie trivia games." The loss of center stage and the bright lights is deeply painful and saddening for them, in the opinion of Cooper. Emotionally these child stars now feel cheated. Angry, they would like to demand a restoration of their lost star status.

A Personal Inventory

We could go on and on, of course. But the only really pertinent questions for me are these: Am I possessed and dominated by things? Where have I invested my heart? Have I so given my heart to a personal gift or to a piece of property that my capacity to love others, to be concerned for their needs and available to their requests, is proportionately diminished? These are questions, I think, that all of us who devoutly wish to be included in the Kingdom of God must ask ourselves. A test exercise which I devised for myself has helped me considerably. Perhaps it will prove to be of some help to you. Maybe you will find out as much about yourself in this process as I did about myself.

Directions: Imagine that God says to you: "I would like the freedom to give you or to take from you anything I please, according to what I see as best for you. However, you may make a list of ten 'untouchables.' List the ten possessions that you most cherish, the ten possessions you regard as most essential to your personal happiness. These I will leave untouched. I will not take them from you."

What would you list? Your listing of these things need not be in order of relative importance, but if you can easily manage that, so much the better.

On the general principle that it is not wise to ask another to do what you yourself are unwilling to do, I would like to share with you my own list of "untouchables." However, it might be good for you to make your own listing before you read the things that I have listed. And when making out your list, please remember this: The fact that you regard something as important to you does *not* imply hands that are unwilling to open. The question of excessive attachment to the things we list is a subsequent investigation. So for now, simply list the ten "untouchables," the things that have the most meaning and importance in your life. After you do this perhaps you will be interested to compare your list with mine.

*   *   *

As I was compiling this list I asked myself this question: Of all the things that are part of "the world" as I experience it, which would be the hardest for me to give up, to be without? Which of the gifts in my life do I regard as most important to my happiness? Here is my list:

1. Mental and emotional health
2. Physical health, especially eyesight
3. Faith and the meaning it gives to my life
4. My sharing in the priesthood of Jesus
5. Membership in the Society of Jesus
6. The nearness of several friends with whom I can be totally open and feel totally safe
7. Love of beauty and the gift of self-expression
8. The acknowledgment of others that I am a sincere and caring person
9. A sense of success: the knowledge that I am actually accomplishing at least in part what I would like to do with my life
10. A sense of humor and the spirit of enthusiasm

The Bottom-Line Question

Now to the critical, subsequent questions: Have I so invested my heart in any of these "untouchables" that I am diminished in my capacity to love myself, my neighbor, and my God? Am I ready to open my hands to God, saying, "Thy will be done!" or am I rather insisting that God let me have my way and my will? Is there something on my list that I simply couldn't live without? This business of open hands is neither simple nor easy. For myself, I would expect that if God did in fact ask the surrender of one of my "untouchables," I would experience my own agony in the garden. However, I hope that with God's grace I could say, as Jesus did, "Nevertheless, not as I will but as you will. Thy will be done." I know that I can manage this only "with his grace"; I know I could not do it on my own. Whenever I read the story of the rich young man in the Gospels, I feel an easy and quick empathy for him. He was invited to go sell all that he had and to follow Jesus. It was no doubt the opportunity of a lifetime, but he was sad because he had many possessions. I feel very sad for him because he missed the opportunity of his lifetime, but at the same time I think I understand something about his sadness. In my own way I think I have experienced it.

God's Tests in Our Lives

Once a brother priest told me that shortly before he was supposed to be ordained to the priesthood, he took a tranquilizer prescribed by a doctor to relieve the tension of "ordination jitters." By a strange biochemical irregularity, for him the tranquilizer proved to be a stimulant. He returned to the doctor and reported the deterioration of his condition. The well-intentioned doctor consequently doubled the dosage, and soon the young man's vision became clouded and his nervousness seriously worsened. Aware of these developments, the superior of the seminary called him into his office and sympathetically but firmly informed him that he could not be ordained.

My friend told me that he went to his room, knelt down at the side of his bed, and thrashed his arms down across the bed again and again, protesting, "Oh, God, you can't do this to me. You can't take thirteen of the best years of my life and then, within arm's reach of ordination, take it all away from me!" The agonized protest soon became a litany: "You can't . . . you can't . . .!" Finally, exhausted and emotionally spent, he fell across the bed and whispered, "But, of course, you can. You can do anything you choose to do. You are my God. I am your creature. Thy will be done."

Then he added something that I did not anticipate: "It was the first time in my life that I had ever experienced complete peace. There were still many unanswered questions throbbing in my head, but my heart knew only the peace of surrender." Later, as the pages of the calendar were turned, the painful questions were answered in time and the young man was granted his desired goal of ordination. But the lesson of peace in the open hands of surrender will be with him all the days of his life.

Something similar once took place in my own life. In a sense it continues to happen in my life. In my early twenties, I visited an eye doctor, an ophthalmologist, for the first time. He seemed to be looking into each of my eyes, searching with his small beam of light, for a very long time. Finally, he stood back and, not looking at me, he asked if I knew about the condition of my eyes. When I responded that I did not, he said softly and somewhat sadly, "Someday very probably you will be blind."

The immediate result in me was an earthquake of shock. Like a sudden crack of lightning, I experienced a thousand painful emotions. No doubt the poor doctor sensed these reactions. Sympathetically, he told me that I was suffering from an inherited, congenital decomposition of the retina, called *retinitis pigmentosa*. He told me that there was no certain prognosis. Many people with this disease, he explained, are already blind at my age. Some have partial vision all their lives. Then he added that I would probably receive some warning in the gradual loss of peripheral vision and the increase of night blindness. "If and when you have only 'tunnel vision,' I would strongly advise that at that point you learn braille before you go blind."

I remember the heaviness and the fear, the grief of anticipation over the possible loss of vision. Leaving the doctor's office, I remember walking down the sunlit street trying to memorize all the visual beauty of that spring day. "Learn braille before you go blind . . ." played repeatedly on the tape recorder of my mind. I wondered how long it would be before I could no longer see the blue sky, the white clouds, the green leaves and grass, the faces of the people I love. I wondered what it would be like to make life's journey by night, stumbling around in a dark world. I recalled also a very emotionally stirring picture I once cut out of a magazine and saved. It was the picture of a blind man, with white cane and tin cup, feeling along Park Avenue in New York City. The sign he wore read, "Please help me. My days are darker than your nights."

Of course, God has asked the surrender of vision from many other people. Some who are afflicted with my disease have been blind since childhood. For various reasons some people are born blind. They have never seen the sky, the clouds, the color green, the radiance of spring-time, and the solemn, sad beauty of autumn. They have never seen the faces of those they love. But here was God warning me that he might ask me to return this precious gift of sight. Here was God asking me to hold out to him my own open hands.

I have often thought that the most common cause of our human inner turmoil is conflict of desires. Our highest expectations and our deepest desires are always struggling with reality. We conceive our own desires, make our own plans, and then hope that there will be a yellow brick road leading straight to fulfillment. Sadly, such success is often not in the script. We stumble and fail to achieve, we lose the contest we wanted so badly to win, and we have to give up the things we would so much like to keep. I have often wondered what it would be like if I wanted only the will of God, if I really took Jesus seriously, if I were really blessed by being poor in spirit, if my hands were open and held out in the readiness to surrender, if . . . "Is it really better to have the Pearl of Great Price or to give it away?"

Just as God did not ask the surrender of the priesthood from my friend, he may not ask my vision from me. It has been thirty years since the original diagnosis, and my vision is still adequate. However, the impairment of vision that I do experience, the loss of peripheral vision and the limitations of night blindness, is a daily reminder: The fullness of personal peace can be experienced only in the full surrender of my will and my desires to the will and desire of God. This is the theology of dispossession, the emptiness waiting to be filled by the presence of God. This is the price and the reward of open hands.

The Clenched Fists: Our Ability to Enjoy God's Gifts

But there is also a question at the other end of the spectrum. It is the question of clenched fists, the theology of possession. I am convinced that God wants us to use and to enjoy the beautiful world that he has made, to join him in his pronouncement: "It is very good!" You and I have to reflect upon our vision of the world and ask about our capacity to enjoy, to find God's goodness in the good things of creation. In the rabbinical wisdom of the Talmud, there is a warning that "every person shall be called to account for all the permissible pleasures that he or she failed to enjoy." A startling statement, isn't it?

Jesus does remind us that we are pilgrims passing through this world, that this is not our lasting city. He assures us that in the end we shall be judged on how well we have loved. However, while warning us not to become attached to the good things we will experience along the pathways of our lives, Jesus does urge us to use and to enjoy these good things. We are to "find God" in all these things.

Virtue, the Romans used to say, stands in the middle. We must be able to use and to enjoy, to experience God's beautiful world of creation without ever being dominated by any of God's creatures. We must always remain free, never letting any thing own us or make our decisions for us. Such cherished freedom is possessed only by the poor in spirit, the people of open hands. The middle ground is this: to use and to enjoy, to experience and to admire God's world (the clenched fists) and at the same time to remain free from the domination of any creature, so that the love of our hearts may be given to God, our neighbor, and ourselves (the open hands).

An analogy may help. Imagine the early American pilgrims, landing on our eastern coast and setting out for California on the western coastline. As I see it, there could well have been two major temptations. The first would be to find some place in the sun, to settle there, and to give up all hope and intention of going all the way to the planned destiny. In this case they would make a permanent settlement at some half-way station. The difficulties of pressing on to their destiny would, in this case, lead them into compromise. This would be like the clenched fists without the open hands. We are pilgrims, too. The Lord tells us that we do not have here a lasting city. He warns us not to gamble on or to give our hearts away to the things of this world, good as they are in themselves. In the end, at the moment of our dying, we must leave them anyway. They are not our final destiny. So while passing through and enjoying this delightful and beautiful world, we must remain ready to give them up. We must be ready for the dispossession of open hands.

79

On the other hand, the early American pilgrims might have been so intent on getting to California, so preoccupied with the thought of their final destiny, that they could easily have missed the enjoyment of all the beautiful scenery along the way: the hills and the valleys, the rivers and the streams, the beautiful sunlit forests. In a similar way, we Christians can be so seriously intent on getting to heaven that we might miss the beautiful world that God has made for us. It is possible that we might not look at creation with the same satisfaction with which God beheld the work of his hands: "It is very good!" This would make our lives on this earth sad and weary but worst of all joyless. This would be the open hands without the clenched fists. This would be the practice of dispossession without ever having possessed the experience of God in this beautiful world which he has made.

God's Creation: "It Is Very Good!"

In the long history of Christian spirituality there have been various emphases. It is true that some of the saints so stressed the detachment of open hands that there is little in their writings about the joyful experience of God's creation. Fortunately other saints have described what has been called an "incarnational spirituality." In his Incarnation, in becoming a man and living in our world with us, Jesus underlined and validated the goodness of creation. Like us in all things, sin alone excepted, the incarnate Word of God was repeating the spoken Word of God at the dawn of creation: "It is very good!"

Saint Francis of Sales (1567-1622), in his effort to redress the imbalance of the puritanical Jansenists, speaks beautifully of the daily joys of Christian living. Saint Alphonsus Liguori (1696-1787) follows in the same "incarnational" tradition. More recently, Abbot Marmion (1858-1923) has insisted that we are humans, and that therefore we must love God in a fully human way. Saint Ignatius of Loyola (1491-1556), in his Jesuit rule, instructs his followers to "seek and find God in all things." Consequently, it is no surprise that this incarnational approach is beautifully developed in the writings of contemporary Jesuits like Karl Rahner, Bernard Lonergan, and Pierre Teilhard de Chardin. It is also reflected in the beautiful poetry of Gerald Manley Hopkins, the Jesuit poet.

Incarnational spirituality seeks and finds God present in all things. Jesus has come among us that we might through him have the fullness of life. Commenting on this, Saint Iranaeus insists that "the glory of God is a person who is fully alive!" We give glory to God by using all the gifts that he has given us and using them to our fullest capacity. We have already mentioned that a part of this fullness is being fully alive in our senses, in our emotions, in our minds, and in our hearts. If the unexamined life isn't worth living, as Aristotle once observed, then the unexperienced universe isn't worth living in. Most of all our Christian faith encourages us to be alive in our hearts. As Antoine de Saint-Exupéry says, "It is only with the heart that one can see rightly; what is essential is invisible to the eye." It would be an unbearably cold world if we passed through it without loving.

Fearing the Full Experience of Life

Sometimes I ask myself which is harder: the clenched fists that reach out to grasp life or the open hands of freedom through detachment. It is indeed a clear-minded and a strong-hearted person who can enjoy without being enslaved. Such is truly a fully alive person. However, this great accomplishment is possible only if we remain open to the full experience of living.

In the book *The Denial of Death*, for which the author won the Pulitzer Prize for Nonfiction in 1974, Ernest Becker suggests that all of us have a "concealed psychosis." In popular usage, a psychosis implies a separation from reality. A psychotic person is commonly referred to as insane. Becker contends that by a camouflaged psychosis all of us cut ourselves off from some part of reality. We cut down and shave our world, and consequently our human experience, to a size which we think we can handle. We cut ourselves off from those things which, if we did not build our walls of separation, might flood into our lives, submerge and drown us. The fear of not being able to cope with the full experience of living results in the tunnel vision of a concealed psychosis.

According to Becker, one such part of the reality which we commonly refuse to confront is death. Most of us have no idea how we would react to impending death because we just don't want to think about it. And just as we fear the end of our finite existence, death, Becker maintains that we also fear the full experience of life. One integral part of a human life is the experience of pain—our own and that of others. However, when someone cries, the most common response is a plea: "Don't cry." It is probably good for people to cry, but most of us don't know how to handle tears. I can't cope with your pain, so I hand you some soft tissues and ask you not to cry. It is a supposed favor to you, but it is actually a request to spare me from full contact with your reality, which at this moment appears to be hurting.

When we cut off the experience of pain, we also separate ourselves from the full experience of the pleasures and beauty of life. There is so much excitement and stimulation in the world of reality that surrounds us—the sights and the sounds, the light and the darkness, the agonies and the ecstasies of God's world. There is so much, in fact, that we are afraid of it. We are sure that we cannot handle it. We sense that we cannot cope with the charge of such high voltage; we are sure that we would suffer a short circuit. So we shut out much of reality and build a little house by the side of the road, laid back from the heavier traffic and surrounded by a hedge of small bushes. There we live a low-risk existence, with the sedations and distractions we need in order to cope with the limited part of reality we are willing to confront.

It is obvious that you and I do have a limited capacity. We cannot take in all the suffering or all the beauty of our world. No one could rightly ask us to do this. It is rather a question here of using more of the capacity that we do have. It would be a waste of our human potential if we were to paint ourselves into a small corner of life and stay huddled there, frozen by the fear of a larger world and a fuller life.

The Christian Vision: Comfort Zones and Personal Choices

The Christian vision would call us out of such isolation and gently usher us back into the larger world, into the drama of human existence. The Christian vision does not easily tolerate the "comfort zones" of cowardice and escape. The Christian clenched fists take into their grasp the full spectrum of human experience. We are challenged to come alive in our senses to the sights and sounds, the heat and the coldness, the height and the depths, the noise and the silence of God's vast world. The Christian vision challenges us to emotional openness, to a willingness to feel both pain and pleasure, the consolations of love and the desolations of loneliness, the agonies of failure and the ecstacies of success. The Christian mind does not wear blinders, does not construct barricades or plant high bushes around its estate. It knows that somewhere a newborn baby is nestling in its mother's arms, and at the same time somewhere else a human being is sweating and writhing in pain with no hope of immediate relief. Finally, the Christian heart, that alone can see rightly, reaches out to love this world into life.

I must choose this Christian vision. It is the most important choice I will ever make in my life. It is the choice that will truly set me free, but still I must choose it. His beatitudes are the Jesus-formulas for happiness, but I must appropriate them, make them my own, if I am to have a singing heart and a celebrating spirit.

One of the most persistent and widely believed delusions is that one person can make another happy. You cannot confer on me the fullness of life. That has to be my choice. Sometimes in relationships one party can twist himself or herself into a pretzel trying to make the other happy and always without complete success. The fact is that no one can make me happy; nor can I make someone else happy. We each have to do that for ourselves. Trying to educate myself to this fact, I see the sign in my mirror every morning that reminds me, "You are looking at the face of the person who is responsible for your happiness today." The clenched fists that open to the full experience of life are a matter of my own decision, my own choice. If I am to live happily and fully, it will be because I have decided to do this. I have chosen to make Christ's vision my own. I have chosen to join God in his pronouncement about creation: "It is very good!"

The Biblical Imperative: Problems on Both Sides

Again, the biblical imperative: We are meant to use and enjoy the good things of God's creation, but to love only persons. Love persons, use things. For most of us, I would suspect, there are difficulties on both sides. Average people are said to use only about ten percent of their potential to enjoy and to use fully the good things God has given us. However, I would suspect that most of us also tend to clutch our possessions and gifts so tightly that when age or death demand surrender, our fingers have to be pried open. We are not ready to open our own hands.

Jesus compares death to two things: *a bridegroom* coming to claim his bride and *a thief in the night* coming to rob us of our possessions. I would think that whichever of these death will be for each of us depends on our attitude toward this world. If we have used and enjoyed the good gifts of God along the journey of life but never held them tightly as our hearts' treasure, we have maintained the open hands of surrender. In this case death will be the *bridegroom* coming to bring his bride to the eternal banquet of celebration. On the other hand, if we have given our hearts to earthly treasures and possessions, then death will come to us as the *thief* in the night, wrenching out of our tightly closed hands all that we have ever loved. This is the sadness about which Jesus warns us when he instructs us to love persons and to use things.

I have a deeply committed Christian friend who once wrote to me:

> I pray for you each day. And my prayer is that you will never be either rich or famous. Money and fame can so easily seduce us from our Christian calling. When we have a lot of money invested in the stocks and bonds of this world, it becomes so easy to pass over the human interest stories to get to the financial section of our newspapers. I thank God for your vow of poverty. And I do pray that you will be spared "celebrity status." Personal fame is really an inversion for a Christian. No one should ever be famous as a Christian. We should want our Jesus to be well known and famous, not ourselves.

Of course, my friend is right, even though something in me snickers: "With friends like this, who needs enemies?" All of us to some extent experience the seduction of various vanities, and we know that it must be a decision renewed every day, to love persons and to use things, to use and enjoy the good things of God's creation without being owned by any of them.

Letting Life Question Us

Dr. Viktor Frankl suggests that we are forever questioning life. What will today bring? Will I get the breaks? Will people treat me well or harshly? Will the path of my life be a happy or a sad one? Dr. Frankl suggests that it would be much more profitable to let life question us.

And obviously life is, in fact, always questioning us. The intrusion of sadness into our lives asks us if we can grow through suffering. The delights of God's creation are questioning our capacity to enjoy: Do I ever allow myself to be truly and completely happy? Someone who loves us and wishes to help us asks us if we can let ourselves be loved and helped. At times unlovable people enter our lives and their presence poses the painful question, Can we love unattractive, even obnoxious people? When someone we have loved dies, life asks us what we truly think and believe about death. When something small and passing goes wrong, life questions us about our maturity and perspective. In this way there is a constant dialogue of questions and answers into which our lives daily invite us. Our answers and reactions to life's questions are always the result of our attitudes. In every reaction there is a self-revelation.

When I ask myself if I really love persons and use things, the truest answer emerges from these daily dialogues with life. For example, when a small child trudges with dirty shoes across Mommy's newly cleaned kitchen floor to hand her a bouquet of dandelions, the mother's first and spontaneous response indicates the priorities established in her attitudes. Does she say, "Oh, thank you, Darling. You are so good. But we have to remember to wipe our feet before coming in the house, don't we?" Or does she rather explode, "Get out of here and take those stupid weeds with you!" When a teenager calls home and tells Dad that he has had an accident with the family car, what is Dad's first question: "Are you all right? We can always get a new fender, but we could never get another you!" Or does he disgustedly demand, "How much damage this time, Dummy?" When we ask ourselves about our attitudes toward and priorities concerning persons and things, we have to watch ourselves in our actions and reactions. The answers are all there.

Our reactions always reveal our attitudes, for better or for worse. The real question is whether we are ready to listen to and to accept this daily revelation of our own inner depths. If we truly want to get to know the attitudes and the vision that are writing the scripts of our lives, all we have to do is listen to our emotional and behavioral reactions. They will always tell it like it is, if indeed we want to know it like it is.

I remember once preaching a powerful sermon on death. Of course, I was insisting, "If we really believe, what fear would death hold for us?" Death can only bring us to that "joy which eye has not seen, nor ear heard, nor the mind of man ever imagined." Turning dramatically first to the left I asked rhetorically, "O Death, where is your victory?" Then turning to the other side, extending both hands in a demanding gesture, "O Death, where is your sting?" (See Saint Paul, 1 Corinthians 15.)

Suddenly I felt a sharp pain in the center of my chest. It was a remarkable experience. My mouth was rattling off the memorized answers prepared by my head and written into my script, while my stomach was panicking at the thought: "This could be serious. This could even be a heart attack. I could be . . . !" The pain, of course, proved to be momentary, but the embarrassing questions lasted for days. Life was, in that experience, questioning me about my attitude toward death. I have always been amused by my response, by the fact that my mouth and stomach are only sixteen inches apart but do not seem to be connected. And, between you and me, I think that my stomach is more truthful in revealing my atttitudes than my mouth.

When I think about my attitude toward the world, I realize that a whole set of attitudes is in fact involved. There are some things that I could easily surrender in the open hands of a free person; there are others that I could probably surrender only with considerable crunching and pain. As always, I am a fraction: I am partly free and partly a prisoner of my own crippling attitudes.

Security Operations: Playing It Safe and Having Enough

In the last years of my dear mother's life, she suffered from a seriously immobilizing arthritis. There were times when I would carry her up and down the stairs of our family home in Chicago. The routine was predictably regular. We would descend several steps, and then Mother would extend her hand and firmly grasp the bannister. The dialogue that followed always went like this:

"Mama, you have to let go. We can't move unless you let go."

"I'm afraid you'll drop me."

"If you don't let go, I'm going to count to three and drop you. One . . . Two . . ."

Mother always let go after the count of two, and then we could descend several more steps. However, after we had progressed several more steps, we rehearsed the same procedure and dialogue. Mama would grab the bannister and I would warn her of her impending doom if she didn't let go.

On one such occasion, I reflected that the exchange between my mother and myself must be something like the exchange between myself and the Lord. Of course, he's got the whole world in his hands, including me, and he's moving me along to my desired destiny. However, I keep grabbing and holding on to the "security bannisters" that help me feel safe. Jesus reminds me that we can't move as long as I hold on so tightly to the little gifts, possessions, and achievements that are part of my security operation. I hear him clearly asking me to "let go . . . ," but out of my ever-honest stomach comes the painful whimper: "I'm afraid you'll drop me." I am frightened by the prospect of open hands. What if I do say the "yes" of surrender? What will happen to me?

Security is such a deep need in us, isn't it? We have all those trembling and disquieting questions pulsing through our nerves and muscles: What will happen to me if I let go? Will I have enough—enough time, enough money, enough provisions for old age, enough people to care for me, enough intelligence, enough health . . . ? And so I hold on tightly to my security bannisters. They make me feel safe but they keep me stationary. They are an obstacle to grace.

The Lord must smile upon me as I once did upon my dear little mother, who was afraid I might drop her. He must want to meet my nervous, tremulous questions about "enough" with a comforting but challenging, "Trust me. I WILL BE YOUR ENOUGH!"

When we love another person, our love sometimes takes the form of comfort and sometimes the form of challenge. Jesus, who loves us, is both of these for us: a comfort and a challenge. There is an inestimable comfort in his presence and the reassurances of his unconditional love. There is also an endless challenge in his request for trust: "Let go. I will be your enough!" It is the challenge of love, asking for our open hands. There will be so many moments in your life and mine, like the stations along my mother's stairway, when we will let go and experience the freedom of being able to move. There will also be times of white knuckles, trembling fears about personal security, and not enough trust to "let go and let God."

"Love persons, use things!" This is the truth that will set us free if we only put it into practice. We must gamble on the gospel formula for happiness. Putting these insights into practice repeatedly will eventually make them habits, make them permanent attitudes. And then we will be truly Christian because our attitudes regulate our choices and our responses to life. Ultimately our attitudes will dictate the outcome of our lives.

An Irish Legend

Once there was a time, according to legend, when Ireland was ruled by kings and the reigning king had no sons. So he sent out his couriers to post signs on the trees in all the towns of his kingdom. The signs advised that every qualified young man should apply for an interview with the king as a possible successor to the throne. However, all such applicants must have these two qualifications: They must (1) love God and (2) love their fellow human beings.

The young man about whom this legend centers saw the signs and reflected that he indeed loved God and his fellow human beings. However, he was so poor that he had no clothes that would be presentable in the sight of the king. Nor did he have the means to buy provisions for the journey to the castle. So he begged and borrowed until at last he had enough money for the appropriate clothes and the necessary provisions. Eventually he set out for the castle, and had almost completed his journey when he came upon a poor beggar by the side of the road. The beggar sat trembling, clad only in rags. His extended arms pleaded for help. His weak voice quietly asked, "I'm hungry and I'm cold. Would you please help me?"

The young man was so moved by the need of the poor beggar that he immediately stripped off his new clothes and put on the rags of the beggar. Without a second thought he gave the beggar all his provisions. Then, somewhat uncertainly, he proceeded to the castle in the rags of the beggar and without any provision for his journey home. Upon his arrival at the castle, an attendant to the king showed him in. After a long wait, he was finally admitted to the throne room of the king.

The young man bowed low before his king. When he raised his eyes, he was filled with astonishment.

"You . . . you were the beggar by the side of the road."

"Yes," replied the king, "I was that beggar."

"But you are not really a beggar. You are really the king."

"Yes, I am really the king."

"Why did you do this to me?" the young man asked.

"Because I had to find out if you really do love, if you really love God and your fellow human beings. I knew that if I came to you as king, you would have been very much impressed by my crown of gold and my regal robes. You would have done anything I asked because of my kingly appearance. But that way I would never have known what is really in your heart. So I came to you as a beggar, with no claims on you except for the love in your heart. And I have found out that you truly do love God and your fellow human beings. You will be my successor. You will have my kingdom!"

The Legend in Matthew's Gospel: The Last Judgment

This legend from Irish folklore reminds me of the twenty-fifth chapter in Saint Matthew's Gospel. There Jesus is describing the final judgment day of this world.

> "Then the King will say to the people on his right, 'Come, you that are blessed by my Father! Come and possess the kingdom which has been prepared for you ever since the creation of the world. I was hungry and you fed me, thirsty and you gave me a drink; I was a stranger and you received me in your homes, naked and you clothed me; I was sick and you took care of me, in prison and you visited me.' "

At this the just are puzzled. They ask the Lord:

> "When, Lord, did we ever see you hungry and feed you, or thirsty and give you a drink? When did we ever see you a stranger and welcome you in our homes, or naked and clothe you? When did we ever see you sick or in prison, and visit you?"
>
> Matthew 25:34-39 (GNB)

The reply of Jesus, in effect, is this:

I was the stranger by the side of the road of your life. I came to you, not in the majesty and splendor of God, but as a poor and simple beggar. I had no claims on you except for the love in your heart. I had to find out if you could open your hands and heart to the needs of your neighbor. Where your treasure is, there your heart will be, and I had to find out where your heart was.

I have found great love in your heart. And so, you shall have a place in my Kingdom forever. You will possess the joy that human eyes have never seen, that human ears have never heard, that the human imagination has never dared to dream. Come, my Beloved, into your Father's house, where I have prepared a special place just for you.

In the end, on the last day and in that final judgment, one thing alone will be important: On that day we shall all be judged on love. Our eternal destiny will depend on the love that Jesus the King finds in our hearts—the love that opened its hands to give away the things of time, the love that opened its hands to surrender human security and all of its bannisters, to say "yes" to Jesus and to all the members of his Kingdom.

The Vision of the World: A Summary

According to the vision proposed to us by Jesus, the committed Christian will not see this world as a source of temptation and be led to flee from it. The Christian believer knows that all those things which the Lord has made are good. However, while seeking and finding the goodness of God in all things, Christians will never become so wedded to this world through which they are passing that they cannot surrender it in open hands at the request of God or at the need of their neighbor. Christians will be fully alive in their senses, emotions, minds, and hearts. They will reach out to embrace life with all their powers. But always Christians will remain free, free from the domination and enslavement that results when we invert the biblical imperative, when we begin to love things and to use people to gain the further possession of those things. Where our treasures are, there our hearts will be. The Christian saves his or her heart for love and that love is kept for God, one's neighbor, and oneself. In the spirit of possession and dispossession the Christian will then enter into the Kingdom of God.

So, I ask myself: "If I were ever to be arrested for being a Christian, would there be enough evidence to convict me?"

CHAPTER 7

The Christian Vision of God

> *We ourselves know and believe the love*
> *which God has for us. God is love, and who-*
> *ever lives in love lives in union with God and*
> *God lives in union with him. . . . There is no*
> *fear in love; perfect love drives out all fear.*
>   1 John 4:16, 18 (GNB)

Two Exercises and Two Traditions

Back in Chapter 4, "The Christian Vision of Self," you were asked to see yourself sitting in a chair, face to face with yourself. It was an exercise of imagination, an attempt to evaluate your self-image. Before we get into this chapter on God, it might be good to repeat the exercise, but this time you are asked to see Jesus in that chair. So once more, warm up your imagination. Visualize the chair and then see a couple of people well known to yourself come successively and sit in that chair. Finally, let Jesus come and occupy the chair. Now you are face to face with Jesus. Be aware of how you feel in his presence. Notice the way he looks at you. What does his facial expression seem to be saying? What can you tell about his feelings for you from his manner and body language?

In a second exercise you might imagine yourself on your deathbed. You overhear the doctor saying to your family, "It won't be long now. It is just a matter of time. We've done all we can to make him (her) comfortable." What would your thoughts be? How would you feel about meeting God face to face? What kind of judgment of your life would you anticipate? The more vividly you can imagine this scene, the easier it will be to get at your root concept of God, the God in your muscles, fibers, and brain cells, the God of your guts. Each of us has a different concept of God. Based on these two suggested exercises, what would you say about your concept of God? Take some time now to try these exercises.

*   *   *

Christianity has preached, taught, and written about God for nearly two thousand years now. And certainly God has been given many different faces. It all depends on whom you are listening to and at what time in history that person is speaking. There has been a long and undeniably fearsome tradition that has given God an angry face. God is portrayed in this tradition as disgusted and at the end of his patience. This is the so-called "fire and brimstone" tradition that gets a lot of mileage out of the so-called "wrath of God." One approaches this God at his or her own great risk. The demands of this God are so rigid and

91

inflexible that they leave us room for little else besides failure, and our inevitable failures always stir the divine wrath.

A less strong and more recent tradition makes God a buddy-buddy type, a "Dutch Uncle" God. This God is definitely pleasant, bland, and slightly wimpish. He graciously asks nothing of us, but invites us only to be nice, to have a good time, and to hurt no one else in doing our thing. He is called by familiar names like "The Man Upstairs" and "The Superstar." He often resembles a genial George Burns.

The God I Don't Believe In

We have already quoted from the fine book of Juan Arias, *The God I Don't Believe In.* I found the summary at the end so moving that I would like to quote it more fully at this time.

> No, I shall never believe in:
>
> the God who catches man by surprise in a sin of weakness,
> the God who condemns material things,
> the God who loves pain,
> the God who flashes a red light against human joys,
> the God who makes himself feared,
> the God who does not allow people to talk familiarly to him,
> the grandfather-God whom one can twist around one's little finger,
> the lottery-God whom one can find only by chance,
> the judge-God who can give a verdict only with a rule book in his hands,
> the God incapable of smiling at many of man's awkward mistakes,
> the God who "plays at" condemning,
> the God who "sends" people to hell,
> the God who always demands 100 percent in examinations,
> the God who can be fully explained by a philosophy,
> the God incapable of understanding that children will always get themselves dirty and be forgetful,
> the God who demands that if a man is to believe he must give up being a man,
> the God who does not accept a seat at our human festivities,
> the God whom only the mature, the wise, or the comfortably situated can understand,
> the aseptic God thought up by so many theologians and canonists in their ivory towers,
> the God who says, "You will pay for that!"
> the God who says and feels nothing about the agonizing problems of suffering humanity,
> the God whose disciples turned their backs on the world's work and are indifferent to their brother's story,
> the God who does not go out to meet the person who has abandoned him,
> the God incapable of making everything new,

the God who has never wept for men,

the God who is not light,

the God who prefers purity to love,

the God who is not present where [people] love each other,

the God in whom there are no mysteries, who is not greater than we are,

the God who, to make us happy, offers us a happiness divorced from our human nature,

the God who does not have the generosity of the sun, which warms everything it touches,

the God who is not love and who does not know how to transform into love everything he touches,

the God incapable of captivating man's heart,

the God who would not have become man, with all that implies,

the God in whom I cannot hope.

No, I shall never believe in such a God.[1]

I heartily agree with Juan Arias. All of my own instincts resonate profoundly with each of the statements quoted above. I don't believe in the God of fire and brimstone, nor do I believe in the "Sweet Old Man Upstairs" who never makes waves or dares to demand anything of us. Genesis tells us that God made us in his image and likeness, and we seem to have a strong inclination to return the favor, to make him over in our human image and likeness. We make him an angry and mean God; we give him a long white beard and a short temper. Or we paint a sweet pastel-colored patsy-God that can be manipulated to suit our moods and needs. Sometimes I think we don't want a God who would have the nerve to intrude into our lives and plans or suggest that he knows more than we do. "Don't you dare rain on my parade."

God Is Mystery

Something in me wants to insist, "None of the above!" First of all, God is infinite. If we ever think we've got him clearly focused in our mind's eye, the one thing of which we can be sure is this: we are wrong. No graven images or sharply focused photographs of God are possible. Because he is so utterly different from and so far beyond anything we can imagine, God is definitely a God of mystery. Sometimes we rankle at this. We want a God that we can fit snugly into our finite little minds, that we can carry around in our little prayer books. We do not want an ungraspable God. In these moments of struggle with mystery, we forget that if we could fit God into our minds, then we would have to pace back and forth in the prisons of those little minds for all eternity. We would certainly grow tired of such a small God.

We must remember that God made our awesomely complicated and vastly beautiful world by a simple act of the will. Just like that. He

---

[1]Arias, *The God I Don't Believe In* (St. Meinrad, Ind.: Abbey Press, 1973), pp. 196-99.

packed every atom of material with enormous power and potential. He strung beautiful stars across the sky of nighttime, and they still shine to us from millions of light-years away. God knows each grain of sand on the seashores of our lakes and oceans. He knows the number of hairs on every human head. This is indeed a God of infinite majesty and power. The appropriate response would be, as Albert Einstein once suggested, an awesome reverence that bows its head and treads on silent feet.

God is to us like the sky to a small bird, which cannot see its outer limits and cannot reach its distant horizons, but can only lose itself in the greatness and immensity of the blueness. God is to us like the ocean to a small fish, which can never fathom the depths or dimensions of the vastness in which it swims. We should really be grateful and delighted that we cannot contain God in the measured dimensions of our thoughts or master him in the cages of our imaginations. We would be bored with him as we are with a shallow and superficial person about whom there is nothing more to grasp or to understand.

God Is Love: He Only Loves

So the Apostle John chooses dynamic rather than static words to describe and define God. God is like light, like a roaring wind. God is ... *love!* We should be careful to notice that John does not say that God *has love,* but rather that he *is love.* This is the very nature of God. Just as we might say, "John is a man," to indicate John's nature, so Saint John writes, "God is love." God's very nature is to love. Now we know that every being acts always and only according to its nature. And so God always and only *loves.* In a real sense this is all God can do because this is God's nature.

An analogy or comparison may help. It is the nature of the sun to give off warmth and light. The sun always shines, always radiates its warmth and light. Now you and I can stand under the sun and allow its warmth to make us warm. We can allow its light to fill our senses and surroundings with light. However, we can also separate ourselves from the sun, in partial ways or even completely. We can put a sun umbrella, a parasol, over our heads or we can lock ourselves in a dark dungeon where the sun cannot possibly reach us. Whatever we do, whether we stand in the sun or separate ourselves from it, we know that the sun itself does not change. The sun does not "go out" if I lock myself in some barricaded dungeon.

Just so, God is love. Because we are free, we can separate ourselves from his love. We can leave him just as we can leave the warmth and the light of the sun. But God, like the sun in our comparison, does not change because we leave him. God is love and does not cease to love because we have left him. Just as the sun always invites us to return to its warming and enlightening rays, so God is forever inviting us to return to him, even when we have distanced ourselves from the reaches of his love. In a real sense, we can *refuse* the love of God but we can never *lose* the love of God. He does not stop sending out the warm and enlightening rays of his love because I walk away from him. If this were so, God would be letting me decide how he is going to act.

It seems to me that it is something like this. Did you ever want to love someone, to share your life and your joy with another, but your offer was refused and your love was rejected? You always knew that the gift of love can never be forced, so you allowed the person whom you wanted to love to go out of your life, away from you. But, as that person was leaving, you called out, "If you ever want to come back, and I hope you will want to, my love will be here for you. I will be waiting for you with open arms and an open heart." This, I think, is something like God's own reaction when we choose to leave him. It is critically important to understand that he does not stop loving, that he does not become angry and vindictive, anxious to punish us in order to get even. That would be a God made to our human image and likeness when we are at our worst.

I am sure that this understanding of God and his love is borne out in the Parable of the Prodigal Son. Jesus tells us that the father (God) allows his son to leave, but he waits patiently for the prodigal's return. In fact, he longs for the return of his son. In the parable, when the boy does come back, his own life and fortunes in shambles, the father runs down the road to embrace his son. The father quickly arranges a party to celebrate his return. "Get out the rings and the robes. Get some music makers in here. Kill the fatted calf. We're going to have a celebration. My son is home!" At the end of the parable Jesus adds that there is more joy in heaven over the one sinner who returns than over the ninety-nine who have never strayed.

God's Love: Covenanted and Unconditional

It is extremely important to realize that God's love is a *covenanted* and not a *contractual* love. In a business contract, if one party fails to meet its commitment, the second party of the contract is released from all the binding effects of that contract. For example, I promise to pay you five dollars to cut the grass in my yard. However, you do not cut the grass, and so I am not bound to pay you the promised five dollars. It is not this way in a covenant. A covenant implies a promise of unconditional love, a promise that is never canceled. A covenant promises a love that will go one hundred percent of the way at all times, no matter what is the response of the beloved. Covenanted love is not earned or won by the person to whom it is given. It is always a free gift. Covenanted love walks undemanded miles, goes far beyond the demands of justice and reciprocity. Covenanted love is never taken back or withdrawn. Covenanted love is forever.

In our human experience, there is usually very little to help us understand this kind of love. Sometimes we think that only a mother loves in this way. However, our great God assures us: "If a mother were to forget the child of her womb, I would never forget you. . . . I have carved your name on the palms of my hands so that I would never forget you." (Isaiah 49:15-16) "I will never ever leave you, nor will I ever forget you!" (Hebrews 13:5)

The "Wrath" of God and Other Anthropomorphisms

Sooner or later the question always arises: What about the so-called "wrath of God," mentioned in the Bible? Biblical scholars assure us that there is no wrath *in* God. God does not get angry, as we do. The scholars tell us that this "wrath of God," mentioned in the Scriptures, is a figure of speech, an anthropomorphism. In such a figure of speech we ascribe human qualities or reactions to God. And while this particular anthropomorphism was probably intended to emphasize the incompatibility of God and sin, it has too often been used in a misleading way. It is true that we can't choose a sinful life, apart from God, and have a loving relationship with God at the same time. But it is likewise true that our sinning does not change God or arouse wrath in him.

It would be seriously misleading to imply that God gets angry because of something we have done. If that were true, we would be in control of God's reactions, which is unthinkable. It is likewise impossible to imagine that the Jesus who insists that we should love our enemies and forgive without limit would add, "But my Father will be very angry if you don't love him!" The only Father revealed by Jesus runs down the road, takes his son into his arms, and sighs with great relief, "You are home! It's all I have ever wanted. Wherever I am I want you with me, and wherever you are I want to be with you. If a mother would ever forget the child of her womb, I could never forget you!"

Once upon a time I used to think: "If I improve, become more charitable, eliminate my frequent faults of commission and omission, if I pray more and so forth, God will love me more." I am now convinced that this kind of thinking involves a serious misconception of our loving God. It is simply incompatible with a true vision of God. Again, it is making God to our human image and likeness. It ascribes to God that kind of "you have to earn it" type of conditional love with which we humans often pretend to love one another.

I now think that if we were to say to God, "I am going to improve; I am going to be better so you will love me more," God's response would be, "Oh, child of my heart, you've got it backward. You shouldn't think that if you become more virtuous I will love you more, because already you have all my love as a free gift. You don't have to change so I will love you more. I could not love you more. What you really need to know is how much I have always loved you. Oh then . . . then you will really change."

Almost all of our human experience has been with conditional love: "If you change . . . if you do this or don't do that . . . I will love you." So we have to sit with this thought of God's unconditional, freely given love, and think about it for a long time. We have to soak in the realization of God's love in prayerful meditation. The truth of covenant, the truth that God could have made a world without you or me, but that such a world would have been incomplete for him—these are truths that are taken in slowly and realized only with the help of grace. God wanted you and me just the way we are, because . . . simply because this is the you and this is the me he has always loved. God *is* love. This is all God ever does.

The "Punishments" of God and the Fear of God

One more uncomfortable question: Does God punish? Again, I would like to step off from what has been a long and strong tradition in Christian rhetoric and preaching. I don't believe in a vindictive God who punishes to get even with us sinners. However, I do believe that we punish ourselves. When we leave the sunlight of God's love, we grow dark and cold, but this is self-inflicted punishment. I asked the classes I teach: "Suppose I were to teach this course, to offer you all the help and encouragement of which I am capable; but you chose not to do the required work, not to study for the examinations and you flunked. In the end, did I punish you by flunking you, or did you punish yourself by flunking?" Most of my students, I think, immediately see the point. They also see the truth that God does not punish us, but that by our misuse of human freedom we can punish ourselves.

We are free. We are capable of sin. We can choose to reject God and the offer of his love. And such choices have inevitable effects. Our sins always result in some suffering. When we leave the sun, we grow dark and cold. Still, we know that the sun is not punishing us for our absence. If we choose to be without God, because we want something more than we want God, we will begin hurting. However, it would be unfair to say that God is hurting us. We cannot truthfully accuse God of punishing us for our failures.

It is even possible that the final choice of our lives, what has been called the "fundamental and final option," is to be without God. If death comes to finalize this choice, we can even lose God forever. In the Gospels Jesus warns us repeatedly about the possibility of this worst of all tragedies. But even in this case, the loss of our souls is the result of our own choices rather than God's punishment. God, who has carved us on the palms of his hands and who will remember us even if our mothers should forget, wants to be with us and have us with him forever. It is God's will that all of us be saved. (See 1 Timothy 2:4.) God is the father of the prodigal, always wanting and hoping for our return.

If we choose otherwise, it will have to be our choice. It can never be his. He can only accept our choice.

Finally, what is to be said about the "fear of God"? It is only a logical conclusion, I think, from what has already been said, that we might very well fear *ourselves.* We can fear the results of our human weakness, the misuse of our freedom in making deformed choices, but we need not fear our great and loving God, who wants only our happiness and salvation. One does not have to fear a mother or father whose love is unconditional and never withdrawn. One of the scriptural images employed to express God's love for us is that of the love of an ever-faithful bridegroom for his bride. We, the bride, can and perhaps should fear the possibility of our own unfaithfulness. The fact is that we are all sinners. We have all been adulterous brides at times. We have been unfaithful to someone who has always been faithful to us. These times of unfaithfulness in my own life I deeply regret. And I do very much fear the possibility of recurrence. Leaving love is the saddest and greatest of tragedies. But I could never believe in a God who demands that I fear him. I could never believe that God is inviting us into such a relationship.

Knowing God by Knowing Jesus

In fact, we have God's word for this. We have the Word that was with God from all eternity, the Word that is God: Jesus. Saint Paul calls Jesus "the visible image of our invisible God." (Colossians 1:15) Theologians have called Jesus our "window into God." And Jesus himself assures Philip, "Whoever sees me sees the Father." (John 14:9) Also, Saint John writes in his prologue:

> The Word became a human being and, full of grace and truth, lived
> among us. We saw his glory, the glory which he received as the
> Father's only Son. . . . No one has ever seen God. The only Son, who is
> the same as God and is at the Father's side, he has made him known.
> *John 1:14, 18 (GNB)*

God not only was in Jesus, reconciling the world to himself (see 2 Corinthians 5:19), but was also revealing himself to us in Jesus. God was speaking our human language, as it were, in becoming a human being, like us in all things except sin. In uttering his Word into the world God was telling us everything he could about himself. The divine person of Jesus is the surest way to a more accurate attitude toward God, even though we can never hope to have a totally adequate view or concept of God. Again, it is obvious that God is simply too big, too magnificent, too infinite for the finite lenses of our minds. However, we can get clearer and clearer insights into the mind and heart of God by reflecting on the mind and heart of Jesus. The wisdom and power, the might and majesty of God reside in Jesus. Through Jesus they are revealed to us.

Jesus and the Law

Jesus began his rabbinical career at the appropriate age: thirty. He was by profession a rabbi. The word means "master," an honorific title that was accorded to the teachers of the Law. (See Matthew 23:7-8.) Consequently, Jesus was expected to give most of his time to the work of interpreting the Law. Rabbis were customarily consulted about questions of the Law. They would inform their questioners about the requirements of the Law in given cases that were presented to them.

A bit of historical background might help here. After the Babylonian Captivity (587-539 B.C.), the Jewish people were allowed by Cyrus the Persian, who had conquered the Babylonians, to regroup. At this time, in the five hundred years preceding the birth of Jesus, the regrouped Jewish people wrote down the Old Testament, including the Torah or laws regulating the life of Israel. These laws were a part of the covenant between God and his People. However, in this period the Law was given a new interpretation and a different emphasis. It became something of an ironclad and absolute norm, and for many of the people replaced a personal relationship with God. The Pharisaic tradition carried this absolutizing of the Law to exasperating extremes. The Pharisees actually started a new tradition. They added oral laws designed to interpret, apply, and preserve the Law by creating new, minute, and very exact precepts. In other words, they embroidered the Law with innumerable, straitjacketing regulations.

When Jesus came into this scene to begin his rabbinical career, the fireworks of confrontation were almost immediate. Jesus kept saying that God is love, and that God is calling us into a relationship of love, not a legalistic relationship with himself. Jesus insisted that the prescriptions of the Law can never replace a personal relationship of love. He further taught that the prescriptions of the Law are elevated, sublimated, and summarized in the law of the love of God and one's neighbor. (See Matthew 22:34-40.) Jesus made it clear that he had not come to do away with the Law, but to bring it to fulfillment and perfection in love. (See Matthew 5:17-20.) The first strategy employed by the Pharisees in dealing with this reluctant rabbi was an attempt to make him solve cases.

"Master (Rabbi), if a man's oxen have fallen into a ditch on the Sabbath, is he allowed to pull them out?"

"Master, are we supposed to pay taxes to Rome? How do you interpret the Law in this matter?"

"Master, how is it that your disciples pick the heads of wheat on the Sabbath when the Law prohibits this?"

"Master, we have caught this woman in the very act of adultery. In our Law Moses gave a command that such a woman must be stoned to death. Now, what do you say?" (The Gospel goes on to say that they asked him this in order to trap him. See John 8:1-11.)

These were some of the "cases" which the Jews asked Jesus to arbitrate in an attempt to make him a legalistic rabbi. As the Scribes and Pharisees asked Jesus to judge the women taken in adultery, he stooped over and started writing in the sand. An old Christian tradition suggests that he was writing in the sand the secret sins of the accusers. More recently it has been suggested that he was so bored with all this self-righteous haggling that he started doodling in the sand in an effort to find something more interesting to do.

What Jesus was saying to the Scribes and Pharisees was very important for them and for us: "You can keep the Law without loving, but you cannot really love without keeping the Law." The Pharisees, who were the most influential group among the Jewish people, could not handle this. They were quite complacent about themselves, and they rather openly despised fellow Jews who were not Pharisees. They called them the "people of the earth," the common people. Generally the Pharisees thought of them as ignorant of the Law and incapable of its observance. The Pharisees believed that these common people were therefore destined to perdition.

Jesus and Sinners

Jesus became even more objectionable to the Pharisees because by association he aligned himself with these common people—with the tax collectors, the prostitutes, the outcasts, and every kind of sinner. He seemed to prefer and to seek out their company. (See Matthew 9:9-13.) The Pharisees were outraged: "He even eats and drinks with sinners!" they gasped.

> One day when many tax collectors and other outcasts came to listen to Jesus, the Pharisees and the teachers of the Law started grumbling, "This man welcomes outcasts and even eats with them!" So Jesus told them this parable:
> "Suppose one of you has a hundred sheep and loses one of them—what does he do? He leaves the other ninety-nine sheep in the pasture and goes looking for the one that got lost until he finds it. When he finds it, he is so happy that he puts it on his shoulders and carries it back home. Then he calls his friends and neighbors together and says to them, 'I am so happy I found my lost sheep. Let us celebrate!' In the same way, I tell you, there will be more joy in heaven over one sinner who repents than over ninety-nine respectable people who do not need to repent."   *Luke 15:1-7 (GNB)*

Jesus was trying to tell them about the infinite love and mercy of God, which was being lived out in him and in his life. But he was also trying to tell them something else. He was saying that the observance of the letter of the Law can kill the spirit of the Law, which is the spirit of love.

If one keeps the Law, keeps from all wrongdoing and legal infractions out of self-righteousness, because he or she is "above that sort of thing," such a person is like a "whitened sepulcher." He or she may be shiny-white on the outside, but inside, if there is no love, there can only be death and corruption. Somehow I am sure that the words "whitened sepulcher" were spoken with more disappointment and sadness than anger in the voice of Jesus. He was asking them, "Please don't be like that. Don't waste your life in that charade."

If you and I could locate ourselves in this Pharisee-dominated scene, if we could feel the shock waves of such reactions to the message of Jesus, if we could listen to the small-town gossip, I think we would have heard something like this:

> "Did you hear what he said when we asked him about his apparent weakness for the wicked, about his softness on sin? Did you hear? He actually said that he was 'the Divine Physician.' Honestly, that's what he said. He said he came 'to care for the sick, not the well.'"
>
> "I once heard him say that he is the 'Good Shepherd.' Are your ready for that . . . the Good Shepherd? He claims that he is in search of his lost sheep! Just who does he think he is?"
>
> "Well!" they huffed. "I've never heard anything like that!"

Simon the Pharisee

One of them, a Pharisee named Simon, had a great story he liked to repeat. Simon had tried a patronizing gesture. He had invited Jesus and a few of his friends over for a dinner. Of course, he did not extend to Jesus the simple courtesies of an honored guest, for example, like washing his feet. Why should he? Jesus should have been happy that he even received an invitation from a respected Pharisee. Well, things were going along pretty well until . . .

> "You won't believe this. In comes a woman [they were never allowed at such banquets]! But I don't mean a woman; I mean the 'town tramp,' a common prostitute! I'm not fooling. This harlot staggers in and stages a big scene. She slobbers all over his feet, and then begins wiping away those phony tears with her bleached hair! [See Luke 7:36-38.]
>
> "Of course, I wondered why this good rabbi didn't kick the slut in the face and chase her away. No, he just reclines there and lets her carry on. It was really disgusting! You won't believe this next part. I cleared my throat as a little hint, and so the Good Master asks me a riddle. Honestly, a riddle! 'If two men owed a third man debts, one a large debt and the other a smaller one, and the good-hearted third man wipes both debts off his books, which would love him more?' Well, of course, I had to go with the one who owed the larger debt.
>
> "Then he really outdid himself. Do you know what he asked me? He asked me, 'Do you see this woman?' I kid you not, he called her a 'woman.' She ought to be stoned to death because she is rotten and

vile, and he asks me, 'Do you see this woman?' Then he proceeds to praise her for the love she has shown him. He says that her sins must be forgiven because no one can show such love unless God is in that person. All love, he says, is a gift from God.

"But here's the zinger: He concludes his little speech by saying that wherever the story of his life is to be told, down through the centuries and out to the ends of the earth, the story of 'this good woman and her kindness to me' will also be told. Did you ever hear anything like that? What a megalomaniac, eh? He obviously thinks that his story is going to live after him, to be told for some years to come!"

Simon's story was only one of many like it. There was a general consensus of opinion.

"He's making a mockery of the Law. He keeps insisting that the Law has been subsumed, elevated into the one great law of love! And you notice how he keeps talking about love, not sin. He is actually trying to imply that God loves sinners. And all of us know that God has only contempt for sinners. What a rabbi, soft on sin and he even eats and drinks with sinners! He is corrupting everything we stand for."

The Proposed Final Solution: The Death of Jesus

Then for the first time someone spoke of a "final solution" to end all this madness. Someone actually said, "Maybe we will have to kill him. It may be better that one man should die than that our nation should perish." The word was sweeping through the whispering galleries that he had raised a man named Lazarus from the dead. Everybody was talking about the power of miracles in his words and in his touch.

So the Pharisees and the chief priests met with the Council and said, "What shall we do? Look at all the miracles this man is performing! If we let him go on in this way, everyone will believe in him, and the Roman authorities will take action and destroy our Temple and our nation!" One of them, named Caiaphas, who was High Priest that year, said, "What fools you are! Don't you realize that it is better for you to have one man die for the people, instead of having the whole nation destroyed?" . . . From that day on the Jewish authorities made plans to kill Jesus.   John 11:47-53 (GNB)

Jesus met their deepest suspicions head on: "Do you think that I am preaching a watered-down, a superficial and diluted version of our responsibilities to God, that I am not demanding enough? When you see me seeking out those who have gone astray, do you really conclude that I am soft on sin? Don't you know that it is possible to love a sinner while regretting the sin? Really, what I am saying is that the observance of the Law without love is lifeless. Relating to God in a legalistic way is like playing a game with God. We make all the right moves and say all the right words, and in the end we proclaim to God with great self-satisfaction, 'See, I kept all your rules. I did everything I had to do. Now

102

you can't damn me!' My Father is not inviting you into such a relationship. My Father loves you. My Father is love!''

Jesus was trying to explain to them that we deal in such a legalistic way only with someone we fear. We feel better when we are covered by the legalistic agreement with all of its clauses and provisions. We meet all that person's requirements, and then we can feel safe and satisfied. However, Jesus was insisting that God is rather calling us into a relationship of love. God is not like a demanding teacher who is intimidating his students with the fear of failure.

Love Is More Demanding Than the Law

The heart of the answer of Jesus is this: Love will ask much more of us than the Law could ever require. When a person enters into a legalistic relationship, that person can come to the point where he or she says, "I have now done enough. I have fulfilled all my obligations." The person can then prove it by citing chapter and verse in the provisions of the contract. However, true love can never say, "I have done enough. I have now fulfilled all my obligations." Love is restless, drives us on. Love asks us to walk many miles not demanded by justice or legalism. In effect, Jesus was saying, "When I confront your legalism with the law of love, I am not asking less. I am not diluting the demands of your relationship with God. Pan-scale justice can only regulate a human life; love will encompass and energize that life. And in the end, love is the only response that you can appropriately make to the loving invitations of my Father, who is love."

I think that Jesus was asking the people of his generation and is today inviting us to drench our minds and spirits in the knowledge of God's love for us. We are the delight of his smiling eyes, the children of his warm heart. God cares for us more than any mother has ever loved her child. If we could only realize how much we are loved, we would of course want to respond, to make some return. "What can I ever do for the Lord in return for all the things he has done for me?" the psalmist asks in Psalm 116. When we have opened our minds and hearts to God's love, we will go far beyond the requirements of what we have to do. Justice and observance of the Law say that I must go just this far. Love will ask me to walk many undemanded miles beyond that point. If we love, we will want to do more than what we must. We will want to do all we can. Love is like this.

In the end, this effort to bring about a *metanoia,* the challenge to acquire a new outlook, proved futile with the people and the powers that prevailed in the generation of Jesus. So one day, near the end, they came to him. They did not try the usual questions of entrapment, but placed before him a direct accusation and a direct question. The accusation was that Jesus was too tolerant, too soft on sin, even going so far as to eat and drink with sinners. The direct questions: "Are you really suggesting that God would approve conduct like yours? How does God think of and treat a sinner?" Jesus looked long and sadly into their eyes, and then responded by telling them a parable: the Parable of the Prodigal Son.

The Parable of the Prodigal

In a parable, two things are put side by side for the sake of comparison or contrast. A parable invites the listener to reflect on the comparison, so that the object or person in question can be illustrated and better understood by reason of the comparison. For example, Jesus says that the Kingdom of God, which he is trying to explain, is like "a man who goes out in his fields to sow seed." (See Mark 4:3-9.) Jesus invites the listener to see a scene from everyday life. By imagining the farmer at work, planting a harvest that will be some time in coming, the listeners could be helped to understand that the Kingdom, the seed of God's invitation, will meet with a gradual, slow-in-coming response of humankind.

One other note to supply context for the Parable of the Prodigal. The most shocking word that Jesus had ever used in all his dialogues with his contemporaries was the word *Abba*. Jesus insisted that God wants us to call him Abba, a tender name that implies belief in an unshakeable and unconditional love, an understanding and enduring love. Abba is the name a small child calls his or her father, and the name itself summarizes their deep relationship of trust and intimacy.

At any rate, on the occasion of the confrontation of Jesus by the Pharisees, when Jesus was asked who God is and how he thinks of and reacts to sinners, Jesus told the story of the prodigal son. Perhaps we should really call this parable the Parable of the Prodigal Abba, because the central message concerns the father and his prodigal (extravagant), unconditional love.

In the story itself, it seems that a man and his two sons live and work together on a farm out in the country. The younger boy more and more comes to think of his father as outdated, and he gradually comes to be disenchanted with, even to resent, life with his father. He has had it with the chickens in the morning and the crickets in the evening. The boy dreams about the delights of the big city with its darkened lights and wicked delights. One day he comes to his father to demand his inheritance and to announce his impending departure. The father is sad, of course, but he finally gives his son the inheritance. The boy, without looking back over his shoulder, sets off to realize his high hopes and to actualize his daring dreams.

Jesus portrays the father as allowing his son to leave, but the father's heart is heavy with regret. During the long interval of the son's absence, the father sits nightly on the front porch of the farmhouse, watching with sad and longing eyes the road from the city. He cannot forget his son. He will always remember his little boy, the apple of his eye and the delight of his dreams. There will always be a special place in the heart of the father for his son. Only when the boy discovers the hollowness of his hopes and the delusion of his dreams, only when his inheritance has been spent and his friends desert him, does he come back down the long road homeward. He is hoping to be hired on as a farmhand, never daring to ask for reinstatement as a son.

Jesus pictures the father, looking as usual down the road that leads from the city, and suddenly recognizing the distant figure of his son. The father's heart pounds wildly, almost breaking with excitement. Overcome with joy, contrary to all the traditions of the time, the father runs down the road and gathers his lost boy back into his own finding arms. He doesn't even hear the boy's suggestion, "I can't hope that you will take me back as a son." After saying this, the boy feels the tight arms of his father encircling him, and hears the relieved sobs in his father's chest. He feels his father's warm tears washing down the furrows of his own cheeks. The father moans softly, over and over again, "You're home . . . you're home!" Then the father gathers himself together, summons his loudest voice, and calls for rings and robes "for my boy." He gives an instruction to call in the music makers, to kill the prized fatted calf. There will be a party to end all parties. He repeats the joyful proclamation: "My son is home! My son is home!"

At the conclusion of this parable, Jesus looks squarely into the eyes of the Scribes, the High Priests, and the Pharisees. "This," he adds, "is who God is. This is how God feels about and reacts to a sinner." (See Luke 15:11-32.) Of course, his story sealed his fate. They would now set into motion the machinery of his death. It would come as no surprise. Jesus knew all the time what the result would be even before he started his parable. And he would gladly die for love. "I have a baptism wherewith I am to be baptized and I am anxious to see it accomplished." (Luke 12:50) Under every crucifix commemorating his death, the followers of Jesus might well see an indelible caption: "This is what I mean when I say 'I love you!'" And down through the arch of the centuries, and out to the ends of the earth, the story would be told and the message would be repeated, and people would gradually come to understand: *God is love!*

Jesus Lives His Message

We have already suggested that when the Apostles were first called by Jesus, they were very far from being finished products. If Jesus had eventually written them out of the script, history would probably have looked back with understanding. The Apostles seemed so slow to grasp his message, to accept his vision, and to honor his values. We have already noted the frequency of the question of Jesus: "Are you yet without understanding?" On one occasion Jesus sighs with relief, "At last, you really understand, don't you?" (See John 16:31.)

The problem was neither lack of intelligence nor lack of goodwill. I suspect that the Apostles ran an average race in these fields. As with most of us, the real problem was *metanoia,* a change of outlook, a new vision. The Apostles had their own dreams, as we have said. They had made their own plans. They were sure about what would make them happy: personal importance, an earthly kingdom, a little security. They weren't asking all that much. But they weren't ready to open their hands to the Lord, to make their surrender, to say their "yes." They weren't ready to invest their lives in a Kingdom of faith and love. And the Lord was asking nothing less of them than this. Jesus was repeatedly telling them, by his words and his example, that those who want to be first shall be last. All authority in God's Kingdom is a call to loving service. Don't worry about security, what you will eat and what you will drink and wear. Look at the lilies of the field, the birds in the air. Trust me. I will be with you. I will be your enough!

For the Twelve Apostles, as for most of us, it was a long road to *metanoia.* They did not easily give up their dreams, their plans, and their hopes. In much of their experience, Jesus had been the magnificent Lord who could give the blind sight and the deaf hearing, and who could cleanse lepers. He could even bring the dead back to life, and drive demons out of human hearts. During these bright and exciting days on the center stage of Palestine, the Twelve walked with Jesus, publicly identified themselves as his followers, and cashed in on the intimacy they enjoyed with him.

Then the lights went out and the tides of good fortune ran out on Jesus. The "Hosannas" of Palm Sunday turned into jeers and demands for his death. The Lord of life, with miracles tingling in his fingertips, strangely became the Lamb of God, bruised and broken. The Apostles quickly retreated to the upper room in search of the security that meant so much to them. They barricaded the doors, and talked only in frightened whispers. They anxiously calculated their chances of getting out of all this alive. What if the scourged Jesus should be crucified? What would happen then to them? Would the forces of darkness that killed him want to destroy them also? From Friday afternoon until Sunday morning, they paced back and forth, fretting and sweating in the hot confinement of the upper room.

Then Sunday morning broke, bright and clear and filled with a great surprise. A breathless Mary Magdalene comes pounding on the door of the upper room: "The tomb . . . the tomb is empty!" Peter and young John run to check out her report, and return to the others to confirm the fact: The tomb really is empty. It was the first, small shaft of light in their darkened world. It was the first ray of hope to pierce their despair.

Then the majestic, risen Jesus passes through the barricaded door. All the blood and bruises, the brokenness and ugliness of his dying are gone. He is again the most beautiful among the sons of men. The Apostles had left Jesus alone to endure the terrible suffering of death by crucifixion. But Jesus comes back to them to share his victory over death. He says simply, "Shalom! Be at peace. I understand."

But they do not understand. As was suggested earlier, they conclude that they are suffering from mass hallucination, seeing a specter, a ghost. So Jesus gently invites them to touch him. As a further reassurance he eats their fish and honeycomb. "Shalom!" he reassures them. "Be at peace. I understand."

They must have remembered his story about the farmer and his two sons, the Parable of the Prodigal Son. They must have remembered how the father ran down the road to embrace his wayward, disillusioned son, to welcome him home. The presence of Jesus in that upper room was so much like this story he had told. Jesus had come running down the road from the tomb where he had been laid in death, and he was embracing them with peace and understanding. "Shalom! Be at peace. I promised you that I would be with you. And I am here." It was just like the father in his story: "Wherever I am, I want you to be with me. Wherever you are, I want to be with you. Wherever you go, I will go."

All along, Jesus had been telling the Apostles that God is love. But they had never experienced this kind of unconditional, covenanted love that never quits, that never ever gives up. When they first heard about this love, the Apostles must have thought that it sounded like a myth, too good to be true. And then he came into that upper room and said to them, "Shalom! Be at peace." Perhaps it was at this moment that they really understood: So this is what love really means. So this is who God really is. There are so many things that we know only when we experience them. Apparently covenanted, unconditional love is one of these things.

The Christian Vision of God, As Recorded by John

One of the men in that suddenly bright and hope-filled upper room was a young man, the youngest in fact, the Apostle named John. John lived to a very ripe old age. By that time all the others in that upper room had long since died heroically for Jesus. Their witness had been martyrdom. John's witness was to be that of an old man telling the young people of his time and all the generations to come about Jesus. (This paraphrase of his meaning supplements his actual words.)

> I want to tell you about the Word of life. I want to tell you what I have heard with my own ears and what I have seen with my own eyes. Yes, I have seen the Word and my hands have actually touched him. I want to tell you what I have seen and heard so that you can join with us in the covenant of love that we have with the Father and with his Son, Jesus Christ. I want to tell you this so that you may share our joy with us and that our joy may be complete. (1 John 1:1-4)
>
> I have seen his always faithful goodness through the works of love which he performed. It was a slow process, but we came to believe in

him. We came to believe in the comfort and in the challenge of Jesus. Jesus came to tell us all the things that he had heard from his father. (John 5:19, 30) Jesus kept insisting with us that his Kingdom was a matter of faith. (John 6:29) He invited us to see everything through the eyes of faith. And he asked us to gamble our lives on the only real force in this world, the force of love. (John 13:34-35)

He assured us that he is the way, the truth, and the life, and that if we followed him we would never walk in darkness. Jesus is the truth, the perfect revelation of the Father, and he shares with us the very life of God that is in him. (John 1:17; 14:6; 17:6) Slowly we came to know a God of love because Jesus introduced us to the meaning and the reality of love. He was so patient with us, as we gradually learned to accept a whole new way of looking at things, a whole new vision of reality. We Christians are those who know this truth because we see through the eyes of faith and we have put on the mind of Jesus. (1 John 2:3-6)

It is this truth, this vision that sets us free—free from all the crippling prejudices that wither the human spirit and cloud the skies of the world. The truth of Jesus sets us free from the tyranny of possession by the things of this world. His truth enables us to rise above the weakness of our human nature. (John 8:31-34; 1 John 2:4)

And this is the truth, the only really important truth, the truth about the Father who was in the Son, the Father who is known only through his Son. This is the truth that sets us free and gives our lives meaning, the truth that makes sense of this world and puts a song in our hearts:

"We ourselves know and believe the love which God has for us. God is love, and whoever lives in love lives in union with God and God lives in union with him. . . . There is no fear in love; perfect loves drives out all fear."   1 John 4:16, 18 (GNB)

CHAPTER 8

The Christian Vision
of Suffering

*The message about Christ's death on the
cross is nonsense to those who are being lost;
but for us who are being saved it is God's
power. The scripture says, "I will destroy the
wisdom of the wise and set aside the understanding of the scholars." So then, where
does that leave the wise? or the scholars? or
the skillful debaters of this world? God has
shown that this world's wisdom is foolishness!
For God in his wisdom made it impossible
for people to know him by means of their own
wisdom. Instead, by means of the so-called
"foolish" message we preach, God decided to
save those who believe. Jews want miracles
for proof, and Greeks look for wisdom. As for
us, we proclaim the crucified Christ, a message that is offensive to the Jews and nonsense to the Gentiles; but for those whom
God has called, both Jews and Gentiles, this
message is Christ, who is the power of God
and the wisdom of God. For what seems to be
God's foolishness is wiser than human wisdom, and what seems to be God's weakness
is stronger than human strength.*
1 Corinthians 1:18-25 (GNB)

Believers and the Question of Suffering

It has been suggested that most people become preoccupied with
their neuroses and personal problems. Paranoid people keep wondering why everyone is out to get them. Pessimists are constantly trying to
convince the rest of the world that things really do look gloomy. In the
same sense, I think that almost all of us keep probing the subject of
suffering. It has certainly been an intriguing question in human history.
Sometimes I think that we have faced the inevitability of suffering. What
we are looking for is some meaningful explanation of the suffering and
pain that touch our lives. The Book of Genesis struggles with the question of suffering in the persons of Adam and Eve and the sweat-and-toil
suffering endured after their fall from grace. In the same book there is
the record of Cain killing his brother Abel. Why? Also in the Old Testament, the Book of Job groans under the weight of this question: Why
suffering? Jeremiah, who didn't want to be a prophet in the first place,

couldn't understand why God called him to failure and rejection. "You haven't made a prophet of me. You have made a fool of me!" (See Jeremiah 11:18-12:6; 15:10-21; 17:14-18.)

The question of suffering is constantly being explored and discussed by thinking people. In our own times there are many good books that take up this question, including the classic of C. S. Lewis, *The Problem of Pain*. Another of these books, the title of which seems significant, is Philip Yancey's *Where Is God When It Hurts?* Somehow I think that this title suggests the deepest source of our preoccupation with suffering. For believers, suffering is basically a faith question, I think, a question of God. Do you remember the old argument, the classic syllogism of atheism? It goes this way: God by definition is all-good and all-powerful. If God could prevent suffering but does not, then he is not all-good. On the other hand, if God would want to but cannot prevent suffering, then he is not all-powerful. In either case, the existence of suffering means that there cannot be a God who is all-good and all-powerful. Somehow I suspect that at least a deep part of our preoccupation with suffering is an effort to reconcile the existence of suffering with the existence of a loving Abba-God.

It would be only sanity, hardly modesty, for me to admit right from the beginning that I do not have all the answers. However, I do think that there are some helpful insights that assist us in formulating a Christian attitude, a healthy and profitable way of looking at suffering. In the end we will confront a wall of mystery. Whenever we use our finite intelligence in an effort to understand our infinite God, we are going to collide with the dead end of mystery. God's thoughts simply are not our thoughts. God's ways are just not our ways. In the end, at the wall of mystery, we will hear the small voice in the soft breeze: "Be still and know that I am God!" (Psalm 46:10)

Loving the Questions, Living the Answers

But God is not asking us to silence our curiosity or to cease our probing of this question of suffering. I think we should continue always to turn the question over in our minds in order to gain new insights and find new meaning. I often review the advice of the poet Rainer Maria Rilke:

> . . . be patient toward all that is unsolved in your heart and . . . try to love the *questions themselves*. . . . Do not now seek the answers, which cannot be given you because you would not be able to live them. And the point is, to live everything. *Live* the questions now. Perhaps you will then gradually, without noticing it, live along some distant day into the answer.[1]

---

[1] Rainer Maria Rilke, *Letters to a Young Poet*, trans. by M. D. Herter Norton (New York: W. W. Norton, 1954), p. 35.

112

I think that "loving the question until I am able to live the answer," in this matter of suffering, is a posture of faith. Suffering asks me to live with and to love the mystery of a God whom I cannot fully understand. Suffering asks me to make a submission of faith to this God who urges me at the edge of my pain: "Trust me!" Sometimes we can see by hindsight that our suffering in the past turned out to be for our own good. Sometimes we can see that if things had worked out as we wanted them to work out, the result would have been disaster. But this by no means suggests that we can ever accomplish total understanding. Even if God were to give us the answers right now, we would probably not be able to understand them.

God is working out a plan for our lives. However, we humans often foil his plans and God has to draw good out of our evil, write straight with our crooked lines. According to the blueprints of this divine plan we humans are free and can therefore fail. We can even hurt one another by misuse of our freedom. You and I cannot understand God's thoughts and ways. Why did he make us capable of sin? We can only love the questions and try to live in a trusting submission to mystery. Recently a fine Christian woman said to me, "Do you know what I want to ask God when I get to heaven?" "No," I responded, "what do you want to ask him?" Her answer was: "Everything!"

God's Response to Job's Questions

When Job asked God to tell him the reasons for his sufferings, God's reply was seemingly a strange one. It was not a doctrinal dissertation on the reasons for Job's difficulties nor an explanation of the motives of God for allowing Job to be so tested. This is what Job seemed to be asking for, and, I think, it is basically what you and I want: an explanation of suffering that we can understand. However, God's reply seems rather to take the form of a personal manifestation of God, a kind of vision of God and his infiniteness that is overpowering. The magnificence and the majesty of God are spelled out in a long description of the wonders of God in the creation of this world. Having experienced God in this kind of overwhelming presence, Job says simply:

> I know that you are all-powerful:
>   what you conceive, you can perform.
> I am the man who obscured your designs
>   with my empty-headed words.
> I have been holding forth on matters I cannot understand,
>   on marvels beyond me and my knowledge. . . .
> I knew you then only by hearsay;
>   but now, having seen you with my own eyes,
> I retract all I have said,
>   and in dust and ashes I repent.
> *Job 42:2-6 (Jerusalem Bible)*

There is a Zen proverb: "When the pupil is ready, the teacher will appear." God seems to be saying to Job and to all of us who demand complete and satisfactory answers: "This is not yet the time for answers. This is rather the time for trust. It may help you to trust in my goodness and power in these matters (your suffering) if you can experience me, my goodness and greatness, in the stunning world of creation. Of course, I have the answers you seek, but you are not ready yet. When you are ready, I will give you these answers. 'When the pupil is ready, the teacher will appear.' Meanwhile, be patient. Love the questions and live in trust. Someday I shall share all the answers and all my secrets with you."

Need for a Previous Mind-Set

When we are asked by God to lie on the anvil of suffering, it is difficult to think clearly at that time. Suffering is like a loud and throbbing noise inside us. It is deafening and distracting. Suffering magnetizes all our attention, leaves us no peaceful and prayerful place. It is difficult, if not impossible, to reflect clearly in times of pain. And so I would like to suggest that what we need is a "previous mind-set," an attitude cultivated consciously in our pain-free moments of peace that will help us in our times of suffering.

Such a mind-set or attitude would seem to be built on and related to our concept of God. In answer to Job's questioning, God responds to Job's complaint by asking his own question.

Where were you when I laid the earth's foundations? . . .
Who decided the dimensions of it, do you know? . . .
Who laid its cornerstone
    when all the stars of the morning were singing with joy? . . .
Who pent up the sea behind closed doors
    when it leapt tumultuous out of the womb? . . .
Have you ever in your life given orders to the morning
    or sent the dawn to its post? . . .
Have you an inkling of the extent of the earth?
                              Job 38:4-18 (Jerusalem Bible)

The power of God is awesome, and God himself is the master of his magnificent world. The mind of God can conceive the overwhelming solar system and produce the multicolored beauty of the seasons. The will of God can execute its own designs by a snap of the finger, as it were. In the presence of such awesome power and intelligence, we should reverently take off our shoes, bow our heads, and tread softly. It is this same God who assures us of his loving governance of the world and of his loving providence over our lives. It is this God of majesty and power who bends down to us, especially in our moments of suffering, and asks us for our act of trust in him. In our "previous mind-set," we

114

must stand ready to trust his infinite intelligence and his awesome power, whatever is asked of us.

Today much is being said about "positive imagining." This technique can be a helpful step toward positive thinking and attitude cultivation. It would definitely assist us in the preparation of the previous mind-set which we are discussing. Positive imagining involves a kind of dress rehearsal on the stage of one's imagination. For example, I want to think and react kindly to someone who is consistently obnoxious to me. So I imagine a situation in which I meet this person. I run through a dress rehearsal on the stage of my imagination. I see myself, in the imagined confrontation, being the kind and tolerant person I really want to be. I do not let the other person, who is offensive, decide my reactions. I am by choice an actor, not a reactor. Such an exercise in positive imagining will practice and reinforce the attitude that I want to make my own. And then, when the actual encounter takes place, it will most likely come off just as in the dress rehearsal. Such positive imagining can be as much a help toward positive and healthy attitudes as rehearsals are to the presentation of a stage play.

Our American astronauts were trained to function in the weightless atmosphere of space by practicing in a "simulator." The exact, gravity-free conditions of space were created inside a model space capsule. Here the astronauts went through their various routines. After the actual blastoff from earth and entrance into space, the astronauts were asked by ground control: "How well are you functioning?" The happy response of the astronauts was: "It is just like practice."

In just this way, I would think, it is possible for us to practice the attitude of trust in God and submission to his higher wisdom. We can cultivate a Christian attitude toward death, for example, by imagining ourselves on our deathbeds. Obviously such meditation on death and dying, recommended and practiced by so many saints, is not intended to be an exercise in morbidity. It is rather a dress rehearsal in which we practice the act of trust and surrender which we will all someday be called upon to make. Such practice will make our response in the actual moment of dying much easier. In a similar way, perhaps, we can prayerfully imagine ourselves in situations of suffering. We can reflect that an encounter with suffering is truly an encounter with God who is the Lord of our lives. We can recall in these moments of reflection that God is both tender and loving and at the same time awesome and omnipotent. We can realize and remember that God promises to sustain us in our suffering, to give us strength. Of us he asks only a trusting submission to his wisdom and will. A definite attitude toward suffering can be cultivated in such prayerful practices or rehearsals. Then in those moments when suffering, in one of its many forms, actually does touch our lives and shake our worlds, we will be strengthened by these preparations and this prayerful anticipation. It will be "just like practice."

Suggestions for a Theology of Suffering

Some "theology of suffering" is also a necessary part in the preparation of this attitude. We have to come up with some answers to our questions seeking to reconcile a God who is love with the fact of suffering. First, I think, we have to face the fact that God had many options in his act of creation. He could have created other worlds, including a world without suffering. He could have created us already in heaven, confirmed in grace and filled with the utter happiness of his presence. Why he chose to create this world, the one we know, why he chose to create us free and capable of sin, capable of hurting one another—this, I presume, is a deep part of the mystery of God. The Russian novelist Dostoevski has speculated that this was God's one mistake: to make us free. When I speculate about this choice of God, to create this and not another world, I think I have to admit with Job:

> I have been holding forth on matters I cannot understand,
> on marvels beyond me and my knowledge.

However, I think that we can safely presume that God knew all the details of the world he chose to create before he created it. He did not create blindly. He was not surprised by the world he made. He knew from all eternity that you would be born of your designated parents at a given day, hour, and second. He knew the number of days you would live. He knew the circumstances of your dying. From all eternity he knew the exact number of drops of water in the oceans which he made. Of course, such intelligence and knowledge are inconceivable by our relatively tiny and finite minds. God is, as we believers have always said, infinite and beyond all measurement by human intelligence.

God knew you and me before he formed us in the wombs of our mothers. (See Psalm 139:13-16; Jeremiah 1:4-5.) He knew of our days and of our nights. He knew there would be springtimes of delight and dark nights of lonely anguish. He knew there would be moments of human ecstacy and other moments when we would feel very much alone and when we would wonder if there really is a God who cares. He knew that our gift of freedom would involve the possibility and fact of sin. He knew that evil would touch your life and mine. He knew that he would offer us the grace to overcome temptation, but that we would at times refuse his offer. He knew that he would have to write straight with our twistedness. He knew that he would have to mend our brokenness. Yet, in full knowledge of all these things, God said:

> "Let there be light. . . . Let there be a vault in the waters to divide the waters in two." . . . God called the vault "heaven." . . . "Let the waters under heaven come together into a single mass and let dry land appear." . . . God called the dry land "earth" and the mass of waters "seas," and God saw that it was good. God said, "Let the earth produce vegetation." . . . God said, "Let there be lights in the vault of heaven to divide day from night." . . . God saw that it was good. . . .

God said, "Let the waters teem with living creatures, and let birds fly
above the earth within the vault of heaven." . . . God said, "Let the
earth produce every kind of living creature." . . . God said, "Let us
make man in our own image, in the likeness of ourselves." . . . God saw
all that he had made, and indeed it was very good.

Genesis 1 (Jerusalem Bible)

Someone has said that what we are is God's gift to us, that what we become is our gift to God. It is true that God gives you and me the lumber of our lives, and offers to help us build from it a cathedral of love and praise. In this matter I have to face my own obvious responsibility. I will either use this lumber I have been given as a stepping-stone, or it will become for me a stumbling block. To use another analogy, day by day God gives me new pieces to fit into this gigantic jigsaw puzzle of my life. Some of these pieces are sharp and painful. Others are drab and colorless. Only God, who has planned and pre-viewed the picture of my life, knows the beauty that is possible when all the pieces have been faithfully put into place. I will know that beauty only after I have put into place the very last piece, the piece of my dying.

Finally, no satisfying theological understanding of suffering can be achieved if one considers only this life which we know, in this world which we know. The context of an endless, eternal life must be in the background of any Christian exploration of suffering. What happens in this life, in this world, can never make sense to the inquiring mind. There is no apparent fairness or equal distribution of blessings. But Christians have always believed that this life is a mere dot on the end-less line of our human existence which reaches from now into forever. Saint Paul consoles the church of Rome with this truth:

I think that whatever we suffer in this life can never be compared to
the glory, as yet unrevealed, which is waiting for us.   Romans 8:18

Like Job, I do not have all the answers. After all, where was I when God made the world? But I do have some understanding of trust. And I do trust the God of love who is my Father. I'm sure you yourself must have been in such a situation, when you had to ask another to trust you. Do you remember that you couldn't really explain? You had to ask for an act of trust. Somehow, I think, in this matter of suffering God puts himself in that very position with regard to us. The great and infinite God asks a very limited and finite you and me: "Can you—will you—trust me?"

An Analogy: The Man from Mars

Someone has suggested this analogy, which appeals to me. Imagine that someone from Mars or another distant planet were somehow and suddenly brought into the surgical operating room of one of our hospitals. The Martian might gasp at the inhumanity of what he would see

117

there. He might describe what he saw in this way: "They put some poor person down on a white table. Then they forced a mask over the face of the poor victim. After rendering the person unconscious, masked men cut into his body and took out some of his organs. Their gloved hands were covered with the poor man's blood. It was a cruel and revolting scene."

Somehow, I think this might be a good illustrative comparison. You and I know that the surgeon is trying to save the person's life. However, to someone who does not understand a surgical operation, it could look like the ultimate cruelty. Sometimes when you and I look at the suffering in the life of another, especially if it is someone we love and care about, we might be tempted to interpret as the Martian did. We might completely misconstrue what is going on, and demand to know why God allowed this to happen. A life-saving, a soul-saving operation of God might look to us like the ultimate in cruelty. In a sense, God deadens us, cuts into our lives, puts in and takes out parts of our selves and possessions of our lives. Just as we entrust ourselves to the surgeon's knowledge and skill, so we are called by faith to an act of trust in and submission to God's infinite knowledge, power, and love. Such an act of trust and submission is obviously a posture of deep faith. I remember reading about the reaction of a mother whose son had been killed by an assassin's bullet. In the depths of her grief and anguish, she expressed the speculation that could have been made only by a woman of great faith. She said, "Maybe if Robert had lived, he might have disappointed the Lord." Such was the faith of Rose Kennedy.

Suffering As a Teacher

Carrying the cross with Jesus is both a posture and a practice of faith. But we can gain helpful insights into the reality and purpose of suffering. The philosopher Proust once suggested that nothing takes a person apart and puts that person back together again, with the result of greater self-understanding, more effectively than suffering. Without any doubt, suffering always teaches us something and often invites us to change and to grow. Again, the Zen proverb: "When the pupil is ready, the teacher will appear." In Chapter 2, "What's in Me?" we proposed the thesis that a distorted and crippling attitude always results in some form of discomfort. I am sure that if we are willing to trace our discomfort to its attitudinal roots, we will usually find the source of our problem and of our pain. Most of the time this discovery will be an invitation to change and to grow.

A physician who worked for many years in a leper colony once philosophized, "Thank God for pain!" The doctor explained that the reason lepers often lose fingers, limbs, and even features of the face is not the Hansen's disease (leprosy). It is rather the absence of sensation, the numbness, the inability to experience pain. A leper might well gouge the flesh of his fingers in twisting a stubborn key in a lock and not really

118

know that he has cut himself. He might not realize that an infection is invading his torn flesh until a finger falls off. He has no sensation, no pain to warn him. Or a leper might hold the very hot handle of a pan over an open fire without realizing that his hand is being burned. He has no sensation, no pain to make him aware of this danger. So thank God for sensation and for pain! They often alert us to the presence of danger and harm. Likewise, the various discomforts we experience may well alert us to our distorted and crippling attitudes. But the lessons of pain can be learned only when the pupil is ready. And this means that we must be ready to enter into our pain, seeking to learn from it. It means that we must repress our instinct to run from pain; we must reject any inclination to drug ourselves into dullness so we won't feel anything.

For example, if people who repeatedly suffer from tension headaches enter into their pain to learn from it, they might well realize that they are unsuccessfully trying to please everyone. It may well be that they somehow attach their sense of self-worth to the approval of others. Consequently, everyone in such a person's life has the power to slash the jugular vein of this person's ego. Or perhaps the tension headaches indicate that the suffering person is a perfectionist, demanding perfection of self and of everyone else. The very possibility of imperfection and failure is a terrifying thought to such a person. Likewise it could be that these headaches result from taking oneself too seriously. Instead of seeing himself or herself as a part of a greater human drama, the suffering person might be seeing self as the only actor on the stage. The whole outcome of the human drama seems to such a person to rest solely on his or her performance. Finally, it could be that the person with headaches is entrusting his or her happiness to others. As we have seen, it is futile for me to make others responsible for my happiness. Happiness is a matter of my attitudes. Happiness begins in the head.

All of the above attitudes are in some way distorted and neurotic. They imply a distorted and damaging way of looking at things. Anyone who consents to live with one of them is doomed to much misery and tension. But notice that the tension headaches are only the symptom, the signal. Pain is the teacher, constantly suggesting a lesson whenever the pupil is ready to listen. Such tension in another person might well take the form of depression or alienation from others. The point here is that the suffering, wherever and however it is felt, is a danger signal, a warning. The suffering is speaking, saying something to the person who will listen. "When the pupil is ready, the teacher will appear!"

Suffering: Its Lessons about Love and Life

Almost all the great figures in the history of psychology have believed that human unhappiness almost always results from a failure to love. When one considers that we must love ourselves, our neighbor, and our God, the truth of this psychological consensus becomes obvious. If a

119

person does not love himself or herself, there is not much that can make such a person happy. There will always be the inner struggle, the inner loneliness, the unavoidable sadness. It is likewise true that if someone does not love others, that person will not be loved by others and will be condemned to live in a small and lonely world. Finally, if someone goes through life without a love relationship with God, much of the meaning of life and the motivation for a life of love will be lost. Such a life journey will be almost meaningless, and certainly old age will be deprived of all hope. The important thing is that suffering is a signal. Suffering, in any of its many forms, is very often underlining a failure to love: either ourselves, our neighbor, or our God. The pain is our teacher, if we pupils are ready to listen. We have to get in the habit of tracing our pain and human discomfort to their attitudinal sources.

A priest friend and confidant once asked me if I was enjoying my priesthood. Of course, I said some inspiring things about my deep sense of commitment and dedication. "Beautiful!" he replied. "However, I did not ask you about that." So I told him about the meaning that I was finding in the exercises of my priesthood. "If I get one thing to do with my life, this is what I want to do!" said I. His reply was presistent: "I'm happy for you, but are you *enjoying* the priesthood?" Perhaps more to my own surprise than to his, I found myself stuttering, ". . . No. I can't say that I am *enjoying* it." He sympathetically added, "You'd better find out why. God can demand heroism of us, but we shouldn't demand it of ourselves."

And so I did my own little investigation of the attitudinal roots of my dissatisfaction. I have already alluded to the discovery of my overre-sponsible "Messiah Complex" and my attitude that tends to exaggerate my own importance. Seeing oneself as the Messiah and as being responsible for the whole world are certainly attitudes that exhaust, drain, and strain the resources of a person. By the way, when I traced the source of my pain to my overresponsible attitude, and when I had exposed my "Messiah Complex," I returned gratefully to my friend. I thanked him for prodding me to examine my lack of enjoyment. I admitted to him, "Do you know what? I was playing Atlas. I was holding the whole world up in my own hands." "Impossible!" he replied. "You couldn't have been supporting the whole world. Do you know why? I was!" Perhaps what we have here is an occupational hazard of those engaged in the priestly ministry.

Suffering Motivates Us to Change

I have for some time been engaged in trying to learn more about alcoholism. The most constant advice I have heard given to the families and friends of alcoholics is absolutely and resolutely to avoid the role of "enabler." "Never cover up for the drinker or clean up his or her messes. Don't try to barter your affection for the other person's abstinence. Don't make it easier for the drinker to live with his or her addiction. Let them feel the pain of their addiction! People change only when the pain gets bad enough!" Of course, I have found this to be true not only with alcoholics but with all of us whose lives need revision. We all have a tendency to stay where we are, even if it is a place of stagnation. It is usually the discomfort or the pain in staying there that jolts us out of our rut toward revision and reform. As the doctor says, "Thank God for pain!" Certainly the most life-transforming insights of my own life have been connected with and have grown out of some experience of pain.

Like the birth of every baby, the bringing forth of human insights almost always involves the experience of pain. I have come to expect that when I enter into my pain rather than run from it, I will find at the center of my pain an amazing insight. Several years ago I remember feeling very angry and upset about a person with whom I had to relate. The very thought of this person seemed to turn my sweetest thoughts into rancid vinegar. I was surprised myself at the depth and dominance of my aversion. A psychologist friend of mine was chatting with me one afternoon in my office. I told him about my strong reactions, my antagonistic feelings with regard to this person. Within minutes he had me looking inside myself for the real source of pain. He reflected, "The world is filled with obnoxious people. When we let them get to us, it is because of something in ourselves." We began to explore my own inner space and in a few moments he saw my shoulders sag with relief. He heard a soft sigh that said, "I've found it!" "What is it?" he asked. "Can you share it?" "Yes, of course," I said. "You see, the Lord has asked me to make my life an act of love. At the crossroads of every decision, if I am to be a Christian, I must ask only this: What is the loving thing to do, to be, to say? And I have committed myself with all my heart to being a Christian. This is my life-wager. However, I have *not* been loving this person at all. I have been wanting to wash this person out of my hair and out of my life. I have not been asking what I might do or be or say that could help this person find happiness and fulfillment. Very simply, I was not loving. The source of my pain is that I have compromised the fundamental commitment of my life."

Several years after that experience, I started to have similar feelings for another person with whom I had to relate. However, the lesson of my previous pain came back as a forcible reminder. Right in the middle of a game of verbal one-upmanship with this second person, I realized what I was doing (trying to win an argument) and what I was not doing (loving). I put up my hands in a "T" gesture. "Time!" I called. Then I openly admitted, "Hey, I'm not loving you. I'm really sorry." So we laughed a little and hugged a little, and have lived happily ever after. Thank God for pain and its lessons. It motivates us to change. And, of course, Jesus was right: "If you make love the rule and constant motive of your life, you will be very happy!"

The psychologists are right, and of course Christian wisdom down through the centuries has always been right about this issue of human happiness. Our unhappiness somehow represents a failure to love. Our suffering and pain remind us, in ways that are difficult to ignore, that our *metanoia* is not complete. We try our own formulas for fulfillment, we put into practice our plans for personal happiness, and we dream our little daydreams of destiny. When these fail, the pain of frustration and the suffering of failure advise us to go back and look again at the gospel sources of beatitude. We have to refocus the lenses of our minds to restore a clear perception of what we are called to be. We must try to come to a clear knowledge that happiness can come to us only as a by-product of love and a life motivated by love.

Suffering and "Contact with Reality," the Reality of Me

It is unquestionable that suffering at times can put us into contact with reality as nothing else can. Sometimes we instinctively slap the face of a hysterical person. The surprise of pain is designed to recall that person from the hysteria back into contact with reality. Physical suffering was once inflicted on mental patients in an effort to call them back to reality. Of course, this proved to be a useless and sometimes a dangerous application of the general principle. But it is a fact that very often our suffering strips us of our pretenses, removes our facades, and forces us out of the roles we are trying to play. Suffering demands that the "real me" stand up to be seen.

I am personally convinced that one of the most common reasons for the failure in love relationships, including the divorce of those who are married, is this: We enter most of our relationships playing a role. We have a sign extended in front of us announcing our role. "I am a helper . . . I am an enabler . . . I am the friendly, smiling type who never gets angry . . . I am pure intellect . . . I am very religious . . . I am the perpetual nice guy . . ." and so forth. The act or role, announced by my sign, is something like a bubble. It marks off "my space." I don't want anyone to pierce or puncture my bubble. In a sense I cordon off "my space" by the announcement and definition of my act.

Obviously, in a truly intimate love relationship, another will come to know me very well. Such a person will inevitably puncture my bubble, will invade my space. Such a person will see that while I like to be a helper, I am also badly in need of help. Anyone who gets really close to me will know perhaps that I smile and don't get angry because I have a terrible fear of being rejected. Such a person will know that I continually smile because I am trying to please everyone. It is the price I am constantly paying for acceptance of others. And oh, I am religious, but I can think and say and even do some pretty irreligious things. Human intimacy exposes all these hidden things in you and in me. In the experience of human intimacy, we are left standing there naked, with all of our warts showing.

122

The pain will be like a two-edged sword. If I confront it, suffering will demand authenticity of me. It will force the "real me" to stand up and be seen. If I enter into the suffering rather than run from it, I can become a real person and have real relationships. Of course, I can run from my suffering, deny it. I can narcotize myself or distract myself so that I won't feel it. Or I can turn my suffering into projected blame, laying the responsibility on others. The sword of suffering, if I refuse to let it cut away my sham and pretense, can even slay me. Suffering can make us either better or bitter. It all depends, of course, on our attitude toward suffering.

Our Pilgrim Status and Our Human Insufficiency

One fact of reality that suffering always drives home is that we are the *pilgrim* people of God. We are on our way home, but we are not there yet. We are only passing through this world. We are in fact moving toward a celebration and a fulfillment that eye has not seen, nor ear heard, nor the human mind ever imagined. It is the joy that the Lord has prepared for those who have loved him. But we haven't arrived yet. This is a fact. This is the reality with which we must live. Our very human temptation is to look for a place in the sun, and to pretend that we have here a lasting city. We want to make of our sunny little hillsides the "mountain of Transfiguration." Like Peter we want to build permanent tents and stay in our cozy little place forever. We want to stop the insistent movement of the clocks and the perpetual counting of the calendars. We want to deny the reality of death. However, the suffering and the pain in our lives won't let us indulge in such daydreaming, in such unreality. Suffering is a constant reminder that we are still en route.

We also have daydreams of our self-sufficiency. We find a strange comfort in the delusions of our personal completeness. We can even hate the thought of dependency because it implies that our personal resources are not sufficient. So we cultivate these dreams of unreality until suffering awakens us. Poor Augustine, after thirty years of running from God, after thirty years of brilliant self-deception, fell on his knees and confessed, "Our hearts were made for you, O God, and they will not rest until they rest in you. . . . Too late, too late, O Lord, have I loved you. . . . The ability to remember is indeed a sad privilege." In a sense, Augustine had to "hit bottom" to be grounded in reality. In his pain and restless emptiness he found his need for the God whom he tried to shut out of his life. Remembrance of the wasted years was very painful, a sad privilege. Almost always suffering has a unique way of unraveling the fabric of our delusions of self-sufficiency. Suffering can make us face and be our true selves as nothing else can. Of course, it is always possible to refuse these lessons, to run away from rather than enter into the meaning and lesson of our suffering. "When the pupil is ready, the teacher will appear."

The Secular Attitude toward Suffering

This Christian attitude toward suffering is obviously disowned and vigorously denied by the world we live in. The message of the media, which is constantly invading our senses and attempting to persuade our minds, is this: go through life with the maximum amount of pleasure and the minimum amount of pain. All suffering must be shunned. Have a happy hour. Desensitize yourself with a few drinks. You only go around once. Grab all you can. Fly now, pay later. Let the good times roll. When in pain, pop a pill. Narcotize yourself. Promote pleasure. Eat, drink, and be merry; tomorrow we die. Remember: This is the "me-generation." Be good to old number one!

To some extent all of us have bought into this "good times" philosophy of life. One needs only to read the statistics to know how successful the world of advertisement and the media have been. In our own country there are enough aspirins and other analgesics sold each year to cure three billion headaches. The most prescribed drugs in our country are the tranquilizers. No other drug is even close. Our little "valley of tears" is rapidly becoming the "valley of Valium." The second biggest business in the country is the illicit production and sale of marijuana. One former user and ardent promoter has said recently, "If you want to shut off your mind, to be really dumb and operate only at a sense level, smoke pot!" Snorting and free-basing cocaine have become the "indoor sport" of many of our idolized actors, actresses, and athletes. More than ten million Americans are addicted to the drug alcohol. One alcoholic told me that he drinks because when he doesn't, life hurts too much. Parents have been led to believe that they are not good parents unless they can keep their children perpetually happy. Throw gifts, food, money, anything at them, but keep them happy!

We are indeed a brainwashed people, ready to scratch before we even have an itch. The advertisers, many of the Hollywood heroes and heroines, and most of the scriptwriters who wash our brains see no value, no redemptive lessons, to be found in suffering. Let the good times roll.

Over and above the smoke of our dreams and delusions stands the loving but lonely figure of Jesus. In back of him, casting a long shadow, is a tall cross. The cross to most of the people in our world is a stumbling block, a madness to be avoided. But to us who believe that there is in suffering the challenge of *metanoia,* the invitation to life transformation and personal growth, suffering is a valuable teacher. Thank God for pain. Jesus seems to be asking our generation, "Can you drink from the chalice of suffering with me? Can you trust me?" And then Jesus says softly, as he did two thousand years ago, "Whoever does not carry his own cross and come after me cannot be my disciple." (Luke 14:27, GNB)

For a Christian there is no other way to maturity, wisdom, and the fullness of life. We must all sit at the feet of this teacher. And we must stake our lives on the surrender of faith and trust that suffering always demands. "I think that whatever we suffer in this life can never be compared to the glory, as yet unrevealed, which is waiting for us." (Romans 8:18)

CHAPTER 9

The Christian Vision
of the Church

God's plan is to make known his secret to
his people, this rich and glorious secret which
he has for all peoples. And the secret is that
Christ is in you.   Colossians 1:27 (GNB)

Another Exercise: The Church Is . . .

At various times I have asked people to do an association exercise
about the Church. It's one of those really simple things. One just com-
pletes a sentence with the first thought that comes to mind. "The
Church is . . ." In my experience, the most common response has been:
". . . a building." Frequent but less common: ". . . an organization run by
priests and ministers" and ". . . where some people go on Sunday." The
responses also get into the school systems, and occasionally a bit of
sadness and bitterness finds its way into the exercises: ". . . a house for
hypocrites." Obviously, there are various ways of seeing or perceiving
the Church. And so we ask: How should a Christian see the Church?
How does Jesus see the Church?

One of my former students, who is now a teacher himself, told me
about a clever teaching devise he uses with his grade school students. It
is meant to get across a simple, clear, and Christian way of looking at
the Church. My friend goes to the chalkboard in his classroom and says,
"I'm going to put the Church right up here, spell it out right here on the
board." So he prints in large letters: CH   CH. Then he backs away,
muttering to himself that "something is missing." Of course, his young
and eager students tell him what is missing: "UR . . . UR!" Then he looks
enthusiastically and points to his young students and exclaims, "Ah! *You*
are at the center of the Church. And so there can be no Church unless
you are there." I rather like that little teaching device. It presents a
bedrock truth in a simple and memorable way.

The Need for the Church

The Church has many facets and can be perceived from many different vantage points. Just as I am a man, a teacher, a priest, a Jesuit and
can be perceived as any one of these things, so the Church can be
perceived as an organism, the Body of Christ, the prolongation of Jesus
in time and the extension of Jesus in space, and so forth. It is undeni-
able that the Church is also an organization, an organization of the

"Jesus People." Just as the organs of our bodies all have specific functions to perform, so every organization has a specific purpose. We don't start an organization and then look for something that it might do. Rather we first have a cause, something to be accomplished, a need to be met. Then we start an organization to work for that cause, to accomplish that goal, to meet that need. Like every other organization, the Church was formed to do something. God wanted something to be done, so he called together a Church, the Jesus People, to do it.

Likewise, all of us are aware that an individual cannot alone bring about widespread change in our world. An individual alone normally cannot accomplish a great cause. So we form political parties, racial equality committees, and organizations to preserve endangered species, to promote respect for life, to preserve the ecological balance, and to promote world peace. An individual who is not fed by the enthusiasm and support of others involved in the same cause usually gives up. Human dedication and enthusiasm for a cause, like everything human, are contagious. Dedication and enthusiasm are caught, not taught. Alone, apart from an organization, each of us would feel lost in the vast human wilderness. Alone we would feel drowned in a great sea of the unconcerned. Alone our voices would be like a soft whisper in the midst of a brass band concert. However, in chorus, the whole world can hear us. So God organized a chorus, the chorus of the Church, because he wanted the whole world to hear the good news.

Assuming these two truths about organizations, imagine now that you are God. (If it comes too easily, don't admit it. People will suspect you.) You are God and you have a cause. You want to gather all the individual human beings whom you have created into one family, your family. They are, as it were, the flesh of your flesh and the bones of your bones. They are made in your own image and likeness. But creatures are not the same as children, and you want to make them your adopted children so that you can share your life, your happiness, and even your home with them forever. You have already decided that these humans, made in your image and likeness, must always be free. And so you will offer your love and your life and your home, but you will not force these gifts upon the children whom you wish to adopt. Now, supposing you were God, what would you do?

What we know is that God himself became a man, and called together a people. He formed an organization. This is the Church. What the members of this Church are supposed to do is to make the announcement, to spread the good news of God's loving intentions to make us his family. This chosen people is meant to invite others into the experience of God's intimacy and into God's family. Sometimes we delude ourselves into thinking that the most important part of such an announcement and invitation is the words we use. Too often we get overinvolved with our words and even lost in them. In fact, the words we use are very often the least important part of the message-invitation entrusted to the Church. There is an old Chinese proverb: "What you are speaks so loudly that I cannot hear what you are saying." All of us know that example is far more eloquent and persuasive than words. When others lecture and sermonize us, we often want to plead with them, "Show me. Don't tell me." People want only values that they have experienced, that they have seen "lived."

And so the most important and effective persons in this Church called together by God are not those who live by preaching, but rather those who preach by living. The most important persons are not the ones who tell us what love is, but rather those who actually love us. And those of us in the Church (like myself) who spend a large part of our lives mouthing the message must admit that words are, or can be, cheap. The true discipleship of a life of love is a far more costly and a far more eloquent testimony. The saints say more by their lives than all the books ever written, than all the sermons ever preached, than all the words ever spoken. However, whatever its diversity of people and roles, the task and function of the whole Church is to bring the human race together as God's family.

God's Cause, God's Plan: To Make Us His Family

This you-and-I Church, then, is God's effort and instrument to fashion for himself a family. Saint Paul calls this cause or intention of God his "plan." Paul says that this plan of God, to make us his family, was hidden in the heart of God from all eternity. Then, Paul says, it was revealed to us in the person and the preaching of Jesus. Finally, Paul insists that it must now be accomplished or achieved through us and among us. (See Ephesians, chapters 1-3.)

What does this plan involve? An adequate understanding would take us all the way back to the very act of creation. Before the world was made, there was only God: Father, Son, and Holy Spirit. In the boundless and infinite ecstasy of their mutual love, they wanted to share what was theirs. Love, of course, always does this. The deepest instinct of love is to share. Love is always self-diffusive. Love has an inner need to give away its possessions. And God is, by Saint John's definition, *Love*. In the act of creation, then, God wanted to share himself, his goodness and life, his happiness and his home. He did not create to get something but to give everything.

By a special choice he picked out each of us for his own. He could have made a world without a you or a me, but this Abba-God didn't want a world without you and me. For him it would have been an incomplete world. Likewise, he could have made us different, but it was this you and this me, just as we are, that God has always loved. He wanted to share himself with this you and this me. However, not only did he want to share *with* us, but he also intended to share *through* us with others. He wanted us to share everything he had given to us individually with our human brothers and sisters.

Gathering a family means that the lines of loving must be horizontal as well as vertical. The reality of a human family clearly involves a vertical relationship between parents and each child. But the love which has its starting point and origin in the parents is also circulated horizontally among the children. The children become channels of love to one another rather than reservoirs which retain what they have in and for themselves alone. Love must flow through the whole network of the family relationship. Eventually such love unites everyone in a family.

Consequently, the love of Abba-God which has been given to you and me is not intended to stop, to accumulate in you and me. Rather it is meant to be passed along through us to one another. No grace of God is really accepted and fully used until it has been shared. There is a saying among the members of Alcoholics Anonymous: "The only way to keep your sobriety is to give it away, to pass it on to others." It is always this way with love. The only way we can keep the love that God has invested in each of us is to pass it on to one another. And it is this that will accomplish God's intention to have us bound together in love as his family. So, of every other human being you and I can truly say, "He ain't heavy; he's my brother. She ain't heavy; she's my sister." And so, God who is Father and Mother to us has made us sisters and brothers in his one family. This is God's cause and God's plan; this is to be the accomplishment of his Church.

The Unity of God's Family

It has often been asked if it really does any good to pray for the dead, to pray to the saints, or to pray for one another. Good questions, aren't they? It seems obvious to me that God could have made this arrangement if he so wanted to. Actually, God can do anything he wants to. The point is that I feel sure that God does in fact make this arrangement because this kind of praying provides interaction and ultimately unity among us. It unites all of us in a network of human interdependency and mutual help. We are indeed God's family, brothers and sisters in the Lord. If one of us is hurting, we are all hurt. If one of us is successful, then we all rejoice. We are family, God's family.

> So then, the eye cannot say to the hand, "I don't need you!" Nor can the head say to the feet, "Well, I don't need you!" On the contrary, we cannot do without the parts of the body that seem to be weaker; and those parts that we think aren't worth very much are the ones which we treat with greater care; while the parts of the body which don't look very nice are treated with special modesty, which the more beautiful parts do not need. God himself has put the body together in such a way as to give greater honor to those parts that need it. And so there is no division in the body, but all its different parts have the same concern for one another. If one part of the body suffers, all the other parts suffer with it; if one part is praised, all the other parts

share its happiness. All of you are Christ's body, and each one is a part of it. In the church God has put all in place.

1 Corinthians 12:21-28 (GNB)

So God has called us together, united us into a people, the family of God, through and in Jesus. Jesus is the vine and we are the branches. Jesus is our God-connection. God's love flows through him and into us, and this life continues to circulate through us and among us. In the beginning, each of us is united to Jesus through the rite of baptism. Through this sacrament, we become parts of his body, live branches of his life-giving vine. We are nourished by all the sacraments, as also by the scriptures, by personal prayer, and by living lives of love. In our Christian living, we begin our family life. We begin to receive our inheritance as the sons and daughters of our Abba-God. We become the heirs of his promise.

In a very profound way we are in fact brothers and sisters to one another. Each of us has already received the first great gift of our spiritual inheritance: the gift of the Holy Spirit. The Spirit of God resides within each of us as the source of the divine life and the source of all the divine graces: peace, power, joy, health, and all the gifts of God. The life of God, which is not fully visible or experiential, is in each of us. From time to time we might experience the touch of God, tugs on our kite strings; but for the most part, we take this on faith. The life of God is in each of us, and this means that we are all closely bonded to one another. We are more closely united by this living presence of the Spirit in us than we would be by family blood lines. The shared life of God, of which we are all temples, makes us family in a very profoundly personal way. This is the faith vision of the reality which we call the Church.

The plan of God then begins with God's generous gifts of life and love. And to those of us who have felt this life and love quicken in us God directs his request that we share with our sisters and brothers what we have received. The reality of the Church, in its most fundamental meaning, describes this network of channels through which the gifts of God run out to all creation. We are the means through which God chooses to bless his world, the means by which God gathers together our human race, to make us his family, and to make us family to one another.

The Church and the Kingdom

Earlier we described the Kingdom of God this way: On the part of God the Kingdom is an invitation to us to come to him in love. On our part the Kingdom is a "yes," a response of love: "Behold we come!" All the scholars of Sacred Scripture are agreed that "The Kingdom of God" is the central message in the preaching of Jesus. The disputed question concerns the time of its coming. Jesus seems to be saying three different things about this. First he speaks of the Kingdom as already present.

> After John had been put in prison, Jesus went to Galilee and preached the Good News from God. "The right time has come," he said, "and the Kingdom of God is near! Turn away from your sins and believe the Good News!"
> Mark 1:14-15 (GNB)

But Jesus also speaks about the coming of this Kingdom as an event that would take place within his own generation. Some of the people to whom he was speaking would witness the coming of the Kingdom.

> And Jesus went on to say, "I tell you, there are some here who will not die until they have seen the Kingdom of God come with power."
> Mark 9:1 (GNB)

In a third set of gospel texts, Jesus speaks of the Kingdom as coming at a day and hour that no one knows.

> "Then the Son of Man will appear, coming in the clouds with great power and glory. He will send the angels out to the four corners of the earth to gather God's chosen people from one end of the world to the other. . . . No one knows, however, when that day or hour will come—neither the angels in heaven, nor the Son; only the Father knows. Be on watch, be alert, for you do not know when the time will come.
> Mark 13:26-27, 32-33 (GNB)

The Timing of the Kingdom: An Explanation

Some scholars have felt obliged to choose one or the other set of texts, reasoning that they can't all be authentic. These scholars then declare the others incompatible and therefore not really the words of Jesus. Most, however, feel that the whole tradition of gospel interpretation moves away from this either-or position. They believe that one and the same Kingdom can actually have three stages in its coming. The Kingdom of God is like a planted seed, which will only gradually reach certain stages of growth. It will achieve these stages only in and with time.

Literally, we know that the Kingdom of God is an *invitation* on the part of God and an act of *acceptance* on the part of our human race. The invitation is extended in a series of requests and events, much as a young man in our culture invites a woman to share his life. There is the first date, the invitation into a special and exclusive relationship ("going steady"), the proposal of marriage, and the engagement period; finally there are the vows and consummation of marriage. In a similar way, God has extended to us through Jesus not one but rather a series of progressive invitations, calling us deeper and deeper into his intimacy.

In the New Testament, Jesus proclaims that the Kingdom of God is here; it is at hand and among us. He is saying that his very presence, as well as his preaching and healing, is itself an invitation into the intimacy of God and into the sharing of God's life. His presence and his works are the first of the three invitations described in the New Testament. Of course, there were other invitations in the Old Testament, made through the patriarchs and prophets.

But Jesus speaks of a time, within a generation, when some of his hearers will see the Kingdom coming in power. Here, I feel sure, he is referring to his death-resurrection-ascension and the outpouring of the Holy Spirit upon the faithful. This would be the second invitation described in the New Testament. Of this invitation, Jesus is in effect saying:

> Within a generation, you will see me hanging on a cross. My blood will run down onto the rocks of Calvary. Oh, but do not mistake this scene for tragedy. No one is taking my life from me. I am offering my life for those I love. My blood will be sealing a new and eternal covenant of love between God and his family. Do not mistake my death for an end. It will really be only the beginning, because I shall rise and will go to my Father. And then he will send the Holy Spirit into the hearts of men and women all over the world. And the Father, the Spirit, and I will take up our residence of love in human hearts.

This intervention-invitation will make possible a whole new dimension of intimacy: God will live and reign in the hearts of men and women as never before. And all this will come as the result of the death of Jesus, within a generation.

Finally, Jesus speaks of the coming of the Kingdom on a day and at an hour that no one knows. He tells the people of his time that they will look up and see the Son of Man coming again on the clouds of the heavens. It will be the end of the world, as we know it. This is the third stage of God's invitation, described in the New Testament. Jesus will call all the just, his people, God's family into the eternal and definitive Kingdom of God. Jesus will gather us all into his Father's house, which we call heaven. And then we will all enjoy forever the deepest intimacy: vision! We will see God face to face, which means that we will know God directly. There we will receive the full inheritance of God's children: his presence, the ecstasy of his happiness, a profound and perpetual peace, the satisfaction of all our desires and the answers to all our restless questions. We will experience forever the pure joy that God has wanted to share with us, his beloved family, from all eternity. This is God's loving plan. These are the stages of God's Kingdom as it is being carried out.

The Kingdom of God, then, is an invitation of God, asking us to enter into, to say "yes" to, and to participate in God's plan of sharing. There are, as mentioned, three major stages of this invitation described in the New Testament: (1) the presence and power of Jesus in the world, (2) his death-resurrection-ascension and the sending of the Holy Spirit, (3) his second coming at the end of the world and the final judgment of the world.

133

Saying "Yes" to the Kingdom

When Jesus asks us to pray "Thy Kingdom come," he is instructing us to ask for the grace to say "yes" to the loving invitation of God who opens wide his arms to gather to himself our human family. Just as there are stages of intervention and invitation described in the New Testament, so there are various stages of intervention and invitation in your life and in mine. Your life and mine are like microcosms of the long, gradual coming of the Kingdom in history. Each life, your life and my life, is a series of interventions inviting a response of love. We have to be ready, to watch, and to pray for one another that we will say "yes" to these invitations spaced throughout our lives. In his book *Prayers,* Michel Quoist writes:

> Help me to say "yes."
>
> I am afraid of saying "yes," Lord.
> Where will you take me?
> I am afraid of the "yes" that entails other "yeses."
> I am afraid of putting my hand in yours,
>   for you hold onto it. . . .
>
> Oh, Lord, I am afraid of your demands,
>   but who can resist you?
> That your Kingdom may come and not mine,
> That your will be done and not mine,
> Help me to say "yes."[1]

I think of this Kingdom in my own life. Each day brings a new supply of "lumber" with which I must build a cathedral of love and praise. Each day brings new pieces of the jigsaw puzzle of my life, which I must fit into place. Each day challenges me to a new, to a deeper and more loving "yes." Some of these invitations are very pleasant, but others are sharp and painful. Sometimes God draws me into a night of suffering and shapes me over the painful fires of doubt. He challenges me forcibly to self-surrender. I feel the ringing blows of his hammering grace on my soul. There are also many invitations that come as spring to melt my coldness. They bring back the grass, the leaves and flowers. The warm breezes of consolation invade my heart. The blood flows again through the veins of my soul.

Sometimes, of course, I am not watching and praying. I am not standing ready with my "yes." So the gracious and forgiving God, who wants me in his family, comes back again to me. He is always the Good Shepherd looking for his stray sheep. He is always reinviting me, asking again for the "yes" of my love and surrender. With Michel Quoist I pray, "Lord, help me to say 'yes.' " And, in the Lord's own words, I pray, "Thy Kingdom come" in my life and in my world.

---

[1]Michel Quoist, *Prayers* (Fairway, Kans.: Andrews & McMeel, 1974), pp. 121, 123.

The "Horizontal" Kingdom

One implication of our call to the Kingdom, which each of us must face, is this: I cannot say my "yes" of love to God without saying my "yes" of love to you. Neither can you say your "yes" to him without including me in your act of love. Jesus is very clear about this. If we come to place our gift of love upon his altar, and while there we re-member that we are nursing a grudge of unforgiveness, we must turn back. We have to make peace with each other first. Only then can we come to him with a gift of self, the "yes" of love. He does not want my gift of love unless it is also offered to you. He does not want your gift of love unless you have shared that gift with me.

> "I have told you this so that my joy may be in you and that your joy may be complete. My commandment is this: love one another, just as I love you. . . . This, then, is what I command you: love one another."
>
> John 15:11-12, 17 (GNB)

In Chapter 5, "The Christian Vision of Others," I quoted the French poet Charles Peguy who reflected that if any of us tries to go to God alone, God will certainly ask us the painful and penetrating questions: "Where are your brothers and sisters? Didn't you bring them with you? You didn't come alone, did you?" In the Kingdom of God I am never less than an individual, but I am never only an individual. I am always a member of a group, called by God to a response of love, which must include the whole group or it is literally unacceptable to God.

The Church is indeed God's family, and the Lord who calls us to a response of love takes as done to himself whatever we do to one another. "Whatever you do to the least of my children you do to me." There can be no relationship of love with God unless we relate to one another in love. Sometimes this seems to be the highest cost of being a Christian. It is so much easier to love the God I don't see than the neighbor I do see. But, as Saint John says:

> The message you heard from the very beginning is this: we must love one another. . . . We know that we have left death and come over into life; we know it because we love our brothers [and sisters]. Whoever does not love is still under the power of death. Whoever hates his brother [or sister] is a murderer, and you know that a murderer does not have eternal life in him. This is how we know what love is: Christ gave his life for us. We too, then, ought to give our lives for our broth-ers [and sisters]! If a rich person sees his brother [or sister] in need, yet closes his heart against his brother [or sister], how can he claim that he loves God? My children, our love should not be just words and talk; it must be true love, which shows itself in action.
>
> 1 John 3:11, 14-18 (GNB)

> We love because God first loved us. If someone says he loves God but hates his brother [or sister], he is a liar. For he cannot love God,

135

whom he has not seen, if he does not love his brother [and sister],
whom he has seen. The command that Christ has given us is this:
whoever loves God must love his brother [and sister] also.

1 John 4:19-21 (GNB)

A God with Skin

There is a well-circulated story about a child wanting to be held by his mother at bedtime. When the mother reminded her little boy that the arms of God would be around him all night, the child replied, "I know, but tonight I need a God with skin on." There is something profound, I think, in the child's reply. There are times when all of us need a God with skin on. Everything that we know in our minds must somehow come through the channels of our senses. Our senses are the organs of our contact with the external world. So, if God is going to come to us through the normal channels of our knowing, he too must somehow enter through our senses. Somehow, God must allow himself to be seen, heard, and touched. In the Old Testament, God's voice is heard in the thunder and seen in the lightning over Sinai. God's voice booms out of the burning bush and out of the mouths of his human prophets. God's is the still voice that comes on the soft breeze, saying, "Be still, and know that I am God." Saint John, at the beginning of his first letter, says that he wants to tell us about Jesus.

> We write to you about the Word of life, which has existed from the very beginning. We have heard it, and we have seen it with our eyes; yes, we have seen it, and our hands have touched it. When this life became visible, we saw it; so we speak of it and tell you about the eternal life which was with the Father and was made known to us. What we have seen and heard we announce to you also, so that you will join with us in the fellowship that we have with the Father and with his Son Jesus Christ. 1 John 1:1-3 (GNB)

The Christians of the early Church knew that all subsequent generations would need "a God with skin." Human beings can encounter Jesus, the source of all life and salvation, only if he is somehow available to their senses. The people of all generations, if they are to meet Jesus, must be able to see and hear and touch him, as Saint John did. It is a fundamental law of human psychology and of human experience.

And this is why God has willed to fashion as his instrument a community of love which we call the Church. Saint Paul said that this plan of God, hidden in God from all eternity, has been revealed by Jesus and must be realized in and through us. Paul exclaims that this is God's plan: *Christ is in us!* (See Colossians 1:27.) God's plan is that Jesus would live on in you and in me and in all the members of his Body, the Church. God would indeed be for all humans in all ages "a God with skin."

136

> God put all things under Christ's feet and gave him to the church as supreme Lord over all things. The church is Christ's body, the completion of him who himself completes all things everywhere.
>
> *Ephesians 1:22-23 (GNB)*

God's plan means this: Jesus will live in each of the members of his Church. This is the way that the people of this and of all generations to come can meet Jesus: in us, in you and in me! We are the flesh and blood, the bones and skin of Jesus, whose members we are. We are God's planned way of sharing himself and his love.

There is a familiar, post-World War II story about a statue of Jesus in the shell of a bombed-out German church. The figure of Jesus was portrayed in this statue as reaching out to the world. However, in the devastation of the bombing, the hands of the statue were broken off. For a long time afterward, the statue without hands stood as it was found. However, a sign was hung from the outstretched arms: "He has no hands but yours!" In a very real sense, this is true. We, the Church, the members of his Body, are his only hands, his only mouth, his only mind and heart. We are indeed the extension of Jesus in space and the prolongation of Jesus in time. We will continue his work of redemption, loving this world into life, or it will not be done at all. The Kingdom of God marches at the pace of our feet.

Of course, this could send shock waves through the nervous system. "I am Jesus to the world? Oh, no! I can't be that." After we get over the initial dread and the impulse to make a disclaimer, I think we all have to realize very calmly that this is not a call to walk on water. However, it is a call to stand up and be counted. Again, we recall the haunting question: If you were arrested for being a Christian, would there be enough evidence to convict you? The Jesus who asks to be recognizable in me isn't the perfect and all-good and all-powerful Jesus. I could never manage that. However, it is rather the Jesus who labors in me, who consoles me and supports me in my human weakness, that must shine out of me. It is the Jesus who said to Paul: "My strength will work through your weakness."

All of us carry the treasure of this loving Jesus, residing within us and working through us, in fragile vessels of clay. We cannot be expected to exhibit perfection, but we must be willing to stand up and to offer our personal testimonials to grace. You and I should want to say to the world, as best we can, by our words and our way of living, by our work and our worship: "Jesus has touched my life. By his kindness, by his encouragement, and by his challenge, Jesus has made all the difference in my life. I was blind and now I see. I was lost and now I'm found!" However, for myself I feel an inner urgency to add to this witness: "But please be patient. God is not finished with me yet."

Stories of Faith: Testimonials to Grace

Today there has been a renewed interest in "stories of faith." More and more people are willing to come forth and tell the world about the touch of the Lord upon their lives. Having no delusions about their personal virtue and perfection, they can nevertheless say with certainty, "He has touched me, and after that nothing was ever the same!" For myself, I think I would be failing in gratitude if I did not say this to the world. No grace is ever fully used until it has been shared. I am certain that the Lord has touched my life, and I do recognize my obligation to share the graces which have been poured out upon me and my life. And so, I want to share God's goodness to me with others, with my sisters and brothers in God's family. Of course, the Lord is not finished with me yet. I am still very frail and flawed. I limp, and I know my own brokenness. I offer no other assurance except to say that I know he has touched and transformed my life.

So, when they ask, "Will the Jesus People please stand up?" I want to stand tall. I want to stand and be counted as one of the Jesus People. But I must share this with you: It would be very frightening to stand alone. I need you to stand with me in the ranks of the Church, the Jesus People. I need my weak voice to be joined by yours in the chorus that sings the Lord's praise and says the Lord's prayer. Yes, I have felt the touch of the Lord upon my life and I have felt the hand of the Lord in mine. But I would be very doubtful about my own experiences if you did not stand at my side and confirm me in my faith by your own testimonial to grace.

Confirming One Another in Faith

I once wrote a small book entitled *He Touched Me: My Pilgrimage of Prayer,* at the request of an editor friend. For many years after the publication of that book, I received several letters each week from various parts of the world. Almost all these letters came from people who were grateful for the gift of being able to recognize their own experiences in mine. It was the joy of recognition, I suppose. "So much of your story parallels mine." It was very consoling and reassuring that the God who has touched me has also touched many others of my sisters and brothers. One of the most moving of these letters was the sharing of a very beautiful and generous woman. She wrote:

> I decided to end my life, which had been utterly selfish and sinful. I was so miserable that I just wanted to end it all. I wanted to die by drowning. I imagined the ocean as a vast and watery mother who would rock me in the cradle of her waves and wash me clean in her waters.
>
> I got to the strand of beach along the ocean, where I was to die. I walked all alone along the deserted shoreline. However, that day the ocean was not a warm and watery mother. The weather was nasty, and the ocean was a snarling beast. Inside me I knew that I had to die,

to end it all. If I had to give myself to a snarling beast rather than throw myself into the arms of a great mother, then so be it.

I had been walking along the sandy beach, and was about to turn into the water when I heard a very clear voice which seemed to be coming from within myself. It was very distinct and clear. The voice asked me to stop, to turn around and look down. There was something irresistible in the command, and so I did as I was asked. I could see only the waves of the ocean washing over, erasing my footprints in the sand. Then the voice returned: "Just as you see the waters of the ocean erasing your footprints, so has my love and mercy erased all record of your sins. I want you back in my love. I am calling you to live and to love, not to die."

It was like a shaft of blinding light in the darkness that was my life at that time. I turned away from the water and from all thoughts of dying. I have, with God's continued love and help, found a beautiful and satisfying life. I am now living and I am loving.

But I have never told anyone, not anyone, what happened to me that day on the beach. My whole life was changed forever by that experience. Still I was afraid that, if I were to share it, someone might tell me that it was all a dream, a delusion. Someone might tell me that I didn't really want to die, and so I made up the voice which would tell me what I really wanted to hear.

Since so much of my life, the good and beautiful life I have found, is built on that moment, I could not risk its sacredness in hands that might be callous and insensitive. I could not bear to let someone take my most sacred secret and ridicule it.

After reading your book, I thought you would understand, and so I wanted to share this with you. You wrote at the end of your book that telling your story was your gift of love to us. Please accept this as my gift of love to you.

Of course, I will never forget that letter, even though I have never met its author. Something about the experience described in that letter sounds very authentic, and the author sounds truly balanced and blessed by God. When I occasionally reread this letter, the whole world seems a bit warmer, the sky always looks a bit brighter, and the loving presence of God in our world and among us seems much more real to me. The Jesus in that woman profoundly stirred in me a thousand remembrances of his goodnesses to me and through me. Her faith and her experience have really supported my own. The story of his goodness to her always starts in me a grateful count of my own blessings. For me she has been indeed, in her act of love, "a God with skin." She was, is, and will always be for me an earthen vessel in whom I have experienced the presence of the Lord Jesus. It was indeed an experience of the reality and the meaning of the Church.

This is the deepest meaning and the fundamental function of the Church, as I see it. As mentioned, the question is not, *What* is the Church? The real question is, *Who* is the Church? "You are" (UR) is the heart and center of the very word *Church*. If we, if you and I, are to be the Church, then I know that I need you, and need you badly, to stand next to me, a God with skin. I need to hear your voice being raised with mine in prayer. I need to know by the experience of your nearness that God has made you my sister, my brother, and that we are together his family. I need to pray with you for the coming of his Kingdom. I need to hear you saying your "yes" which braces my own "yes" with a new strength. There is an inevitable contagion in everything human. And so I need the support of your presence, your love, and your person. God reaches out to me through you and out to you through me. And if, somehow and for your own reasons, you should choose to "leave the Church," please do not think that you have simply walked out of a building or an organization marked with weakness. The fact is that you have left us who need you and who will miss you and your love.

*   *   *

Sometimes some frightening questions surface in me: Is all this a dream, a lovely little fairy tale? Is this community of love which we call the Church a fact or a fiction? Did God really make us in his image and likeness, or have we made up a God of love? Oh, I do believe. I have believed with enough depth and enough strength to wager my life on the reality of the Church. In fact, I resonate very deeply to the words of Jean Anouilh's Becket when he says, "I have rolled up my sleeves and taken this whole Church upon my back. Nothing will ever persuade me to put it down."

Still, there are parts of me that faith has not yet claimed. "Lord," I pray, "I do believe but please help me with my unbelief." I try to love my unbelieving questions until I can live the believing answers. One thing, however, seems certain: Every life must be based on some act of faith. Faith is basically a judgment, a judgment about whether the Word of God is true or not. If faith is a judgment about something for which there is no logical or scientific proof, then sooner or later all of us must make some decision, some act of faith in this matter. We must gamble our lives on something. Not to decide in this matter is really not a clever way to escape error. Not deciding is in itself a decision.

For myself I have made my judgment and my life commitment. I have also reflected that if the love of God, the call of the Kingdom, and the reality of the Church are only a dream, then the opposite would be a nightmare. The opposite judgment or act of faith would see us all as mere animals in search of prey. The strong would then devour the weak. The rich would buy and sell the poor. The handicapped would be destroyed as defective and unproductive. In the end, our only destiny would be to turn into dust and become food for worms.

I am reminded of what Dorothy Thompson, a journalist, once wrote. She was interviewing a survivor of a Nazi concentration camp. During the interview, she asked the survivor if any in those camps had remained human. His immediate reply was: "No, none remained human." Then he caught himself and remembered: "No, there was one group of people who did remain human. They were the religious people." The survivor said that all the others, even those who had great knowledge and skill, seemed to be using their abilities only selfishly for survival. The very architects of those camps had used their great knowledge and skill only to destroy. The knowledge and skills of a technological age without the compassion and wisdom of faith proved in Nazi Germany to be gruesomely dangerous and destructive. In her summary, Dorothy Thompson wrote: "I am beginning to think that when God goes, all goes." Her line was somewhat reminiscent of what George Washington said in his Farewell Address: "Morality cannot be maintained without faith and religion."

I am so grateful for the tugs on the string of my kite. I know that there is a God up there because I have experienced his presence, his power, and his peace in my own life. I have also experienced his presence and love in my sisters and brothers in the Christ, whose Church we are. In the end I must trust my own experience. I believe that Jesus is in us and works through us. I am satisfied with this truth on which I have wagered my life. Somehow I know that it has given me roots and wings: it has set me free.

CHAPTER 10

The Christian Vision of the Will of God

> When Jesus had said this, a woman spoke
> up from the crowd and said to him, "How
> happy is the woman who bore you and nursed
> you!" But Jesus answered, "Rather, how hap-
> py are those who hear the word of God and
> obey it!"   Luke 11:27-28 (GNB)

"Thy Will Be Done"

For a Christian, in a very real sense, the bottom line of life is this: doing the will of God. This is the measure of what we call holiness. And for a Christian this is the only measure of success in life.

The late Padre Pio, the Capuchin stigmatic who bore the wounds of Christ on his body, was reputed to know everything. I once met this saintly man and was convinced by all that I saw and heard that indeed he did have a profound intuition of people; he had the gift of reading human hearts. Believing this, I wrote to him and asked him if he had any special message for me. In his response he said that he did indeed have something special to say to me. As I read this my heart started pounding and I could feel a sense of emotional anticipation rising in me. He wrote:

> The strongest and most effective prayer, which you should make the center of your life, is this: "Thy will be done!"

Somehow I felt disappointed. My heartbeats returned to a normal rhythm, and my emotions sagged back into place. My expectations shook their little heads sadly. I think I expected some clairvoyant statement, some startling revelation about my past or a dramatic prediction about my future. "Thy will be done" just didn't do it. It seemed too basic, too fundamental, too taken-for-granted. It wasn't what I expected or wanted to hear.

I was relatively young at that time, anxious for excitement. As the years have moved on into middle age, I have more and more come to see that this desire to do the will of God is the heart of the matter. Seeking and embracing the will of God is the hallmark of Christian maturity.

I now think that we become adult Christians whenever we move from the position of making our own plans and asking God to support them to the position of asking God honestly and openly, "What are your plans? I'd like to be a part of them." Early on in this book I mentioned a sign over the sink in the room where I live. There are really two signs. My first semiconscious thoughts stir in me every morning when I read these two signs. They remind me of my two basic responsibilities. The first sign reads, "You are looking at the face of the person who is responsible for your happiness today!" The other sign reads, "Good morning, Jesus. Thank you for loving me. What have you got going today? I would like to be a part of it." I often think that this early morning rehearsal of my mind-set is an important part of my effort to become an adult, grown-up Christian. Some mornings I can read my signs with great enthusiasm. Other days the words taste like straw and tend to stick in my throat.

Misunderstanding the Will of God

In the course of my own life experience, it seems that it has always been at the scene of some great or small tragedy that people have brought up the "will of God." I remember some years ago trying to console a woman who was sobbing almost hysterically just after the death of her husband. Unexpectedly someone in that room of grief remarked, "It is the will of God, you know." So abruptly did the woman stop crying that I stood there amazed, silently wishing that I had thought to say that. Now, of course, I realize that it would have been much better to let her release her grief and to express her sense of loss. But, the "will of God" is often used as a bromide to dull the sense of pain and to cover the pangs of grief. The "will of God" is often bottled with the label: "To be taken whenever things get rough."

I think that this crisis application is really a misunderstanding of the will of God. The will of God is, in fact, our happiness. That's why God created us: to share his life and love, his happiness, and even his home with us. It would be a serious misunderstanding of God and his will if we were to associate the will of God only with suffering, loneliness, and grief.

I think there is a usable analogy in the parent-child relationship. Almost all parents clearly want the happiness, the fulfillment of their children. They want exactly what the children themselves want: happiness and fulfillment. What parent and child may disagree about is the *means.* The child may not want to take vitamins or to stay in the safety of the backyard; the child may want to play with matches or sharp knives. At times like these the parents have to step in and assert their wisdom and their wills. The parents want the child to be happy and healthy; the child wants to be happy and healthy. It is only a question of who knows what *means* will best produce that desired state of happiness and health.

Most of the time, I would presume, the wills of parents and children are not in conflict. When Mom and Dad take the children to the beach or circus, when the whole family is eating dessert or playing some game, there is no conflict. Likewise, when God offers us all the good and beautiful things that he has made for our enjoyment, there is no conflict. And we are certainly doing his will when we are enjoying, appreciating, and being grateful for these many beautiful things: for good food, the moon and the stars, white sandy beaches, rippling streams and roaring oceans, the smiling faces of friends, the joy of a newborn baby, the encircling arms of love, the joys of success, the music and the poetry of the universe, rainbows and Christmas trees. God has looked on all these things and pronounced them "very good!" And it is his will that we join him in that pronouncement, that we use and enjoy the marvelous and delightful works of his hands. All this is definitely an important part of doing the will of God.

There are, of course, times when the will of a mother and father will not be the will of the young child. Most of the time, when we are very young, our parents do know what is best. Of course, it would really help if children could be convinced that their parents really do want only their happiness, even when their parents won't allow them to experiment with matches or play in the street or stay up all night. Likewise, it would really help us if we could really believe that what God wants is our happiness, even when he challenges us with difficulties and asks us to endure failure or grief. The comparison between God and parents is valid, I think, except that parents can be wrong in some of their judgments. God, by definition, is infinitely intelligent and infinitely loving. God cannot be wrong. He knows much better than we what will make us happy. God clearly implied this in his question to Job: "Where were you when I made the world?"

A dear and good friend of mine, now deceased, had suffered more ill health than anyone I have personally known. A coronary heart attack at age thirty-five. Multiple surgeries for cancer, which left a gaping hole in the center of his face. This necessitated a prothesis to replace his nose and cheekbones. Because of his consistent ill health, he was greatly limited and confined to sedentary occupations. He suffered prolonged bouts with pain and was often embarrassed by his affliction. Once I asked this man about his reaction. Did he ever get depressed? Was he ever bitter? I will never forget his reply: "These are the cards which God has *lovingly* dealt me, and these are the cards I will *lovingly* play." I will always remember and be grateful for that response of my friend.

God's Will: General and Specific

It is obvious that a necessary part of growing up is the chance to make our own decisions and choices. We will make some of these decisions and choices poorly, and in these cases we will have to learn from our mistakes. This is a part of the growing-up process. Consequently, parents must give their children an increasing liberty to make their own choices as the children grow older. If the mother and father were to dictate all the decisions of their children, the end result would be disastrous. The parents would wind up with indecisive, conformist, emotionally crippled children walking around in adult bodies. People who have been treated this way stumble and stutter through life, asking others, "What do you think I should do?" They hitchhike through life, carried along on the wisdom and maturity of others. All of us must have the liberty to make our own decisions and our own mistakes, to live with them and to learn from them. There is simply no other way to become mature.

So it seems to me that if God had a definite and detailed will for every one of our actions and in all our situations of choice, he would be aiding and abetting infantile delinquency. We would all end up indecisive, immature children, walking around in adult bodies. With our fingers laced nervously together, we would forever be praying to know the will of God. Should I go here or there? Should I paint my house this color or that? Should I locate my office on the second or third floor? The practice of faith, based on the supposition that God has a definite and detailed will for everything we do, would produce childish little robots instead of mature human Christians. God our Father would not do this.

The only reason why a person might find comfort in believing that God does have a definite and detailed will in all things would be that it provides an escape from responsibility. The escapee from responsibility never has to make personal decisions, to take personal responsibility for his or her life, and never needs any inner reexamination of motive and attitudes. For such a person there is a hotline from heaven and all messages come directly from God, who bears all the responsibility. It is the formula for a stagnant life and perpetual immaturity.

My own belief is that God has, in our regard, a *general* and a *specific* will. I think that the general will of God asks us to do something loving with our lives, to glorify God by using all of his gifts to the full. Indeed God has given each of us unique gifts. And he asks us to invest these gifts wisely and lovingly in the cause of his Kingdom. Such a generalized life commandment to make our lives an act of love leaves many decisions up to you and me. In fact, one of the most difficult parts of being a loving person is making all the decisions that love must make: What is the loving thing to do, to say, to be? Love is not a simple matter. I must listen empathically to you and to your needs in order to learn where you are and what you need at this moment. At the same time, I must also love myself and my God. Consequently, I must weigh my own needs against yours. Which are the most urgent? I must also consider the needs of God's Kingdom in most of my decisions. This general will of God that we make our lives an act of love allows us much room for the healthy exercises of maturity.

We obviously need God's *enlightenment* when we are trying to make these decisions of love. And I think that God is most happy to provide the graces of enlightenment. He will help us to see the issues involved in our decisions, issues that we might not have noticed. His grace will help us to gain a needed perspective, to take a longer and wider view, when we are making our choices. But as we go into that final room marked "decision," we must go in there alone. We must exercise and stretch our own muscles if we are to grow. Often we must learn from our mistakes and reverse our mistaken judgments wherever possible. This is necessary for all of us if we are to grow into mature and faithful Christians. When God gives me the lumber of my life and asks me to build a cathedral of love and praise, he does not supply an architect's blueprint, complete in every detail. Rather, his general will simply asks me to make love the rule and the motive of my life.

On the other hand, there may well be times in your life and mine when God will have a *specific* will, a call to something which is very definite. God has a providence over our world and over human history, which I think of as his "master plan." I believe that God has designed a whole network of crisscrossing causes designed to achieve the intentions of his master plan. While we probably live most of our days under the general directive of making our lives an act of love, there will be definite times when God will open a very specific door and ask us to go through it. There will be some deeds and accomplishments which are specifically entrusted to you and to me. No one else can do them.

I believe, for example, that I became a priest in response to a specific call of God. When people have occasionally asked me why I became a priest, I have replied, "If you want my reasons, I will be glad to try to impress you. But the real reasons are not mine. The real reasons are God's, and I do not know them." All I know is that once upon a time God opened a door and his grace moved me through it. He allowed me at that time to think my own thoughts and to react to my own motives. But there was this greater plan, this providence of God over the history and over the world of humankind. In that plan of providence, there is indeed a set of specific things which God has called me to do. Why he chose these specific deeds of love for me or me for them I do not know. I am happy to love these questions until God graciously supplies the answers.

There have been quite a few times in my own life when I have felt the winds of God's grace in the sails of my small boat. Sometimes these graces have moved me in pleasant and sunlit directions. At other times the requested acts of love were born in the darkness of struggle and suffering. There have been springtimes and there have been long, cold winters of struggle for survival. God has come to me at times with the purest kindness, at times with the most affirming encouragement, and at other times with bold and frightening challenges. I think that all of us have to watch and pray, to be ready to say "yes" when God's language is concrete and his request is specific—"yes" in the sunlit springtimes and "yes" in the darkness of winter nights.

Discernment: Through Attraction and Peace

The specific will of God is not always preceded by a great gong and an announcement in solemn tones. Most times we have to prayerfully "discern" or discover this specific will of God. How do we go about this? First, let me say that I think that the only person who can successfully and safely discern the will of God is one who really wants to know and to do the will of God.

There is a story, which I believe to be reliable, about one of our best-known Christian authors. It seems that this man had gone to spend a year in a monastery to deepen his own spiritual perceptions and to find his own spiritual directions. One day this subject of the will of God came up in conversation between the author and the Abbot of the monastery. The author asked the Abbot, "What is the most necessary step in finding the will of God?" The Abbot replied, "The most necessary step to find the will of God in a specific matter is to want the will of God with all your heart in all things and at all times."

The person who is seriously seeking and wanting God's will can trust that God's specific will can be found in his or her own deepest inclinations and attractions. Many of the saints have said that they knew a given action was the will of God for them because they experienced such a strong attraction within themselves for this course of action. Thérèse of Lisieux once said that she knew God wanted her to become a Carmelite sister because he had planted in her heart such a strong desire for this. Again, the main question which you and I must confront is this: Do I really want the will of God? Am I deluded first by wanting to make my own plans and then by insisting that God support and realize them? Or do I seek to find my place in God's plans, in God's "master plan" of providence? If the second, then I can safely and wisely consult my own deepest inclinations and attractions to find the movements and directions of grace.

The second method of discernment which I have found helpful is this. Again, the supposition is that I have made my act of faith and that I truly and above all want God's will. When we come to the frequent forks of decision in the roads of our lives, it is very profitable to imagine ourselves following each of the possible courses of action. Having placed before our minds all the alternatives, the one in which we find the greatest peace of heart most probably is the specific will of God for us.

Why? Imagine with me, if you will, that the grace of God is a physical force. His grace gently moves us in a definite direction. When we try to go in another, contrary direction, we have to exert force and we will feel the friction and the struggle of this opposition. However, if we move with, flow with the gentle but directive force of grace, we will feel rather the support and momentum of the gentle pressures of grace. In a similar way, even though grace is not a physical but a spiritual reality, when we are moving in the direction of God's grace, there is an inner experience of harmony and peace. We are moving with the flow. There is a sense that "this is the right thing to do, to say, to be." On the other hand, when we are "kicking against the goad," as Saint Paul says, there is an experience of struggle. "There is another law warring in our members." The force of our wills is not flowing with the movement of grace, but pushing against it.

In the concrete, when I am trying to find out if there is a specific will or directive of God, more than anything else I have to try to become aware of my own basic and general intention: Do I really want the will of God? Am I willing to suspend or at least hold in check my own desires until I have found out God's desires. Am I ready to open my hands to God? Is my central and strongest prayer, "Thy will be done!" This desire always to do the will of God is the most important part of our discernment. This must always be the deepest desire of our hearts.

Discerning the Will of God: A Summary

You and I have to struggle through these profound and sometimes painful questions. I personally find it very costly to confront myself with the question, What do I really want? We can and we should pray for the grace to want God's will, believing as we do that his will is, in fact, the only way to our own true and deepest happiness. Only when we want God's will before all else can we safely consult our deepest desires and inclinations, trusting that these desires and inclinations have been born of grace.

At the crossroads of love's many decisions, we can place before our minds and hearts the alternatives, the possible courses of action. Wanting God's will, we will find in one of the alternatives greater peace of heart, an inner sense that "This is right!" On the other hand, we will experience some confusion, some inner struggle with the courses of action that are contrary to God's will. I have deliberately chosen the phrase "peace of *heart*" rather than "peace of *mind*" for a definite reason. Most theologians believe that the Holy Spirit works not only in our conscious thoughts but also in our subconscious. Many times the Holy Spirit does not share with our conscious minds all the reasons and motives for a given inclination, but moves us anyway, by forces we cannot recognize or name, to fulfill his higher purposes and to attain our own ultimate destinies. We experience peace when we harmonize ourselves with this movement of the Spirit. The head may be left with a thousand questions, but the heart's intuition will sense that "This is right!" and will know a peace of its own.

Trusting the Lord

There is an ancient directive: "We pray as though everything depends on God but work as though everything depends on ourselves." Another version of the same goes this way: "When you are out at sea and a storm arises, pray with all your heart but row with all your might for the shore."

Recently I heard a story about a man whose house was located in a flooding area. When he looked out the window of the first floor of his house, he saw a man riding by in a boat. The man in the boat shouted, "Get into this boat and save your life!" "No," came the reply, "I am going to trust in the Lord." The floods kept rising and soon the poor fellow was looking out the window of the second floor of his house. Again a man in a boat rode by and implored him to get into the boat and save his life. "No," came the firm reply again, "I am trusting in the Lord." The floods continued to rise. Soon the man was forced to the highest peak of his rooftop. A helicopter flew by and hovered over his head. The pilot said over a loudspeaker, "We're going to drop a rope ladder. Climb into the helicopter and save your life!" Once more the stranded man, perched high on his rooftop, replied, "No, I am going to trust in the Lord!"

Well, it seems that the floods continued to rise and the poor man was eventually drowned. At the "pearly gates" he encountered the stately figure of Saint Peter, snowy beard and all. "Say, I've got a complaint. I want to get it off my chest before I go into heaven. I understand that no one can complain in there. I want to tell you that I trusted in the powers of heaven and you let me down!"

Peter meditatively stroked his long white beard and replied, "I don't know what else we could have done for you. We sent two boats and a helicopter."

Sometimes trusting in the Lord can be used as an excuse for our own reluctance to work as though everything depends on us, to row with all our might for the shore. Wanting the will of God can never be a substitute for personal determination and hard work. We have to get into the boat, climb the rope ladder, use the means of achievement that God provides for us. God helps those who help themselves. If we really will the end, we must also will the means. We should ask God to help us with our work, but not expect him to do it for us. Trusting in the Lord should never be a cloak over our own cowardice or laziness.

Mary: Pietà

In the Gospels (Luke 1:26-38), we read of an angel coming to a young girl with a question she could not have anticipated: "Will you be the mother of the Messiah?" The overwhelmed girl had already promised her virginity to God. She did not understand how she could be a mother. The angel proceeded to assure her that it would not be by the power of man but by the power of God that this would come about. "The Holy Spirit will come upon you."

Gathering her startled wits together, the young girl asks the only important question: "Is this really the will of God? Does God really want this of me?" This had always been her heart's desire: to do God's will in all things. The angel assures her that it is the will of God, and the young girl, Mary, bows her head with an immediate "yes!" "I am the Lord's servant. Let it happen to me as you have said!" (Luke 1:38) And so, in this moment the Word was made flesh. The Son of God took his humanity from her body and from the power of God, took up his residence within her, under her immaculate heart.

When Mary said, "Let it be done!" she did not understand all the other "yeses" that would be inside her first "yes." Scripture scholars do not think she knew that the Messiah whom she had consented to mother would be in fact the Son of God. I am also sure that when she became visibly pregnant, she did not know how to explain her motherhood to Joseph, who was "making plans to divorce her." I think she wondered often about the future of the little baby she held in her arms that night in Bethlehem. Afterward, she did not understand that faraway look in the eyes of her little boy. It was a look that seemed to stare far into the future. It was almost as though he knew of his destiny to do something that would change the whole course of human history. Likewise, I think that Mary was puzzled by his response to her worried question, when he was lost in the temple: "Son, why did you do this to us? Your father and I have been terribly worried trying to find you." He answered only, "Didn't you know that I had to be about my Father's business?" I am sure that Mary did not understand.

However, if heaven is where God is, that little cottage in Nazareth must have been for thirty years a heaven on earth for Mary. It must have been a heaven on earth that she had not dreamed about even in her most glorious dreams.

Then, after Joseph had died (as we presume), Jesus said that he had to leave her, to walk the long and lonely roads of Palestine announcing the Kingdom of God to the people of his time. After seeing him disappear down the road, Mary most probably walked back into that little house in Nazareth alone. There must have been a great emptiness in that house, the kind we experience when we return to our homes after the funeral of a family member. We know from the Gospels that sometime later Mary did celebrate a wedding of friends with him at Cana. She even alerted him to the embarrassment of the newly married couple: "They have no more wine!" Most probably she was puzzled by his reaction: "My hour is not yet come." Of course, she still trusted in the compassion and power she had always experienced in her son, and told the waiters, "Do whatever he tells you."

Apparently Mary was not with him on Palm Sunday. She did not hear the "Hosannas!" or experience the tingling excitement of his public acclamation and triumphant entry into Jerusalem. The final gospel portrait of Mary is the terrifying scene on Calvary. She stands there bravely at the foot of his cross, watching her son die slowly and painfully. And,

151

as the sky darkens, she holds the dead body of her son in her trembling arms.

Michelangelo has carved out of marble a beautiful tribute to this young woman. It is likewise a tribute to her "yes" to God's will. In the statue, Mary is holding Jesus in her arms, looking upon his torn body with a mother's tender and loving compassion. Michelangelo calls his statue the "Pietà." *Pietà* is an Italian word which means "faithfulness." Mary is the woman who with all her heart wanted only the will of God, who said her "yes" but did not understand all that it would involve. But she trusted God, trusted that he loved her, trusted his wisdom and his ways, even when she did not understand. Michelangelo's summary of her incredible achievement is the one word: PIETÀ.

She said her "yes" to God's will, and she was faithful to the end.

The Christian who has really put on the mind of Christ knows that the Lord never really spoke of success, but only of "faithfulness," of *pietà*. When we see our Christian lives in the perspective of the gospels, faithfulness to God's will is the only real, eternal crown of success.

May an angel write on our tombstones, yours and mine, the appropriate epitaph to summarize our lives upon this earth: PIETÀ.

Epilogue Prayer

God, my Father: Create in me a heart that hungers for your will alone—a heart to accept your will, to do your will, to be whatever you want me to be, to do whatever you want me to do.

When you chose to create this world, you knew the blueprint and the design of my life: the moment of my conception, the day and hour when I would be born. You saw from all eternity the color of my eyes and you heard the sound of my voice. You knew what gifts I would have and those that I would be without. You knew also the moment and the circumstance of my dying. These choices are all a part of your will for me. I will try lovingly to build an edifice of love and praise with these materials which you have given me. What I am is your gift to me. What I become will be my gift to you.

As to the future, I ask for the grace to sign a blank check and trustfully to put it into your hands, for you to fill in all the amounts: the length of my life, the amount of success and the amount of failure, the experiences of pleasure and of pain. I would tremble to do this except for one thing: I know you love me. And, of course, you know much better than I what will truly and lastingly make me happy.

In response to your will, I want my life to be an act of love. Wherever there is a choice, help me to ask only this: What is the loving thing to do, to say, to be? To make the decisions that love must, I seek and need your enlightenment. Touch my eyes with your gentle and healing hands that I might find my way along the winding course of love. Strengthen my will and direct my feet to follow that course always.

And whenever there is something special your love has designed for me to do in my life, let me be found ready and waiting. Help me to become a sensitive instrument of your grace. I believe that you have a providential master plan for this world, and I want to be a part of it. I want to make my contribution to your Kingdom, the contribution you have entrusted only to me. I want you to use me to help love this world into the fullness of life.

Finally, my Lord and my God, let me be faithful in my commitment and dedication to your will, faithful until the end. Let "faithfulness" be the summary of my days and of my nights. Let the inscription on my tombstone read: PIETA.

ACKNOWLEDGMENTS *Continued from page ii*

Excerpt from Robert C. Leslie, *Jesus and Logotherapy.* Copyright © 1965 by
Abingdon Press. Reprinted by permission of the publisher.

Excerpt taken from *Prayers* by Michel Quoist. Copyright, 1963, Sheed and Ward, Inc.
Reprinted with permission of Andrews and McMeel, Inc., and Les Editions
Ouvrieres, Paris. All rights reserved.

Excerpt from Rainer Maria Rilke, *Letters to a Young Poet,* trans. by M. D. Herter
Norton. Copyright 1954 by W. W. Norton. Reprinted by permission of the
publisher.

Excerpt from *Tales of a Magic Monastery* by Theophane the Monk. Copyright © 1981
by Cistercian Abbey of Spencer, Inc. Used by permission of The Crossroad
Publishing Company.

Excerpt from Dylan Thomas, "Do Not Go Gentle into That Good Night." From Dylan
Thomas, *Poems of Dylan Thomas.* Published by New Directions Publishing
Corporation and J. M. Dent. Copyright 1952 by Dylan Thomas. Reprinted by
permission of New Directions Publishing Corporation and David Higham
Associates Limited, London.